# Houston Atlas *of* Biodiversity

*Houston Wilderness*

*Texas A&M University Press*
*College Station*

Library of Congress Cataloging-in-Publication Data

Houston Atlas of Biodiversity : Houston Wilderness. –
   1st ed.
      p. cm.
   Includes index.
   ISBN-13: 978-1-58544-618-6 (cloth : alk. paper)
   ISBN-10: 1-58544-618-1 (cloth : alk. paper)
   1.  Biodiversity– Texas– Houston Region.
   QH105.T4H66 2007
   578.709764'1411– dc22
                      2006102653

Houston Wilderness wishes to acknowledge the
following for their generous support of the
Houston Atlas of Biodiversity:

George and Mary Josephine Hamman Foundation
Albert and Ethel Herzstein Charitable Foundation
The Moody Foundation
The Powell Foundation
The Woodlands Development Company

Houston Wilderness would also like to thank the
Houston Advanced Research Center for support of
this publication through management of chapter
content preparation and development of maps and
geographic information systems (GIS) data.

Design and production by Dearwater Design.

Printing provided by ConocoPhillips company.

# Dedication

"When we see land as a community to which we belong, we may begin to use it with love and respect."

*-Aldo Leopold*

We dedicate this Houston Atlas of Biodiversity to the people of the Houston Wilderness region in hopes that they will use our land with love and respect.

# Table of Contents

# Houston
# Atlas *of*
# Biodiversity

# HoustonWilderness

### What is Houston Wilderness?

Natives of the Texas Gulf Coast have always favored the beauty of the land around Houston. Sitting at the intersection of the great and western prairie, the vast southern forests, and the Gulf of Mexico, the southeast Texas region offers enormous ecological and recreational diversity. As the region has boomed with new people and prosperity from the energy, medical and space industries, attention has been devoted to more urban endeavors. As our region matures, it is time to connect again with our extraordinary natural heritage.

Houston Wilderness is a consortium of local, state and federal agencies, research and education centers, conservation organizations, business and economic interests, and individuals devoted to understanding, appreciating and preserving the ecological diversity that is found in a twenty-four-county area of southeast Texas, or a hundred-mile radius around Houston. This ecological diversity has been known for decades to experienced bird-watchers and natural scientists, but it has gone largely unrecognized by the general public and our economic leaders. Houston Wilderness was formed to remedy this gap in awareness about all that lies within about a hundred miles of Houston.

The considerable ecological diversity of the Houston-area landscape was inventoried in the early 1990s in a map prepared by Charles Tapley and Jim Blackburn for an environmental planning class at the Rice University School of Architecture. Titled "Ecological Capital of the Houston Area," the map depicts the location of various ecosystems that surround the Houston metropolitan area like a necklace of jewels (see page 5). Enormously varied, these encompass pineywoods, Big Thicket, forested Columbia and Trinity bottomlands, the prairies, coastal marshes, and bays and estuaries—all ecological systems of note as well as features of the southeast Texas landscape.

Houston Wilderness is committed to the idea that quality of life and the long-term appreciation and protection of these ecological systems are bound to one another. We believe that responsible stewardship of our natural resources enhances the economic well-being of our communities and the mental and physical health of everyone who lives here. We believe there is an increasing need for people to enjoy and experience the opportunities provided by wild places. It is our belief that the long-term benefit of conserving these natural resources leads not only to wealthier economies but to healthier minds, bodies and communities.

We are indebted to Chicago Wilderness for pioneering in the 1990s the concept of an urban wilderness. People in Chicago realized that large county-owned lands set aside long ago had become a significant natural asset for the expanding metropolitan area and, even more important, that these lands are a reservoir of now rare native species of tallgrass prairie plants and insects. Unlike almost all other surrounding prairies, the county lands had never been plowed; the prairies were in pristine condition. Besides being a key recreational resource, they are today the focus of

*A map inventorying the ecological diversity of the Houston area was created by Jim Blackburn and Charles Tapley for an environmental planning class at the Rice University School of Architecture. This map helped fuel the original concept for Houston Wilderness as a region and an organization.*

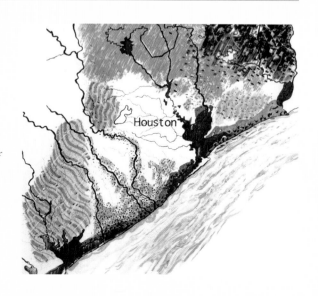

Houston

much research and a source area for prairie restoration work (see www.chicagowilderness.org; and see Sullivan, An Atlas of Biodiversity, in Further Reading at the back of this book).

At Houston Wilderness, we envision a metropolitan area where residents understand the value of conserving and enhancing our cultural and natural heritage. We envision a region with an educational system that promotes a conservation ethic by teaching children about the outdoors, in the outdoors. We envision a community of people who frequently enjoy the nearby national forests, national wildlife refuges, state parks and other ecological destinations. We envision a partnership between urban and wild areas that leads to greater economic prosperity through increased quality of life. Finally, we envision an area that is recognized as an international destination for nature enthusiasts of all ages and backgrounds.

Beware of those who suggest that the countryside for a hundred miles around Houston in all directions is nothing but flat, soggy terrain of no interest, with endless millions of mosquitoes to make your life miserable, and that for almost half the year it is simply too hot to do anything much outdoors anyway. The same people may go on to note that the woods are crawling with dangerous snakes, alligators are a hazard in the bayous, jellyfish will sting you in the surf, fire ants are a routine pest, flooding destroys homes and snarls up highways with depressing regularity, and about once every couple of decades, a big hurricane will roar in from the Gulf and do some appalling damage.

Those who view the local natural environment merely as hostile, and imagine that to enjoy the outdoors you have to head for Colorado or Cancun, are missing out on a great deal.

At the beginning of the twenty-first century, excellent diversity of ecological systems still exists in these twenty-four counties. World-class birding and recreational opportunities abound. It is our

challenge to understand these natural resources better—to recognize the natural capital we have as citizens of this region—and find ways to pass these wild areas on to those who come after us.

## Landscape on the Move

On the Texas coastal plain we can get a good sense of local geological history simply by looking at the ongoing work of rivers and bayous and at the action of waves along the beaches. Many of the processes visible today mirror what has been going on in the region for millions of years.

Rivers and streams and bayous meander and cut; they deposit sediment; and when they flood, which is often, they spread out new layers of sediment stacked upon the old. The result is a wedge of sands and clays beneath us—an extremely large wedge. Under Houston, it is about ten miles thick. This impressive stack of sediments accumulated as material eroded far inland was swept toward the sea, and the shoreline inched outward from an original coastline around Austin. With advancing deposits, that shoreline marched eastward and southward into the Gulf, and as it advanced, the whole mass was depressed under its own weight.

There have been other kinds of movement as well. The great ice age glaciations did not reach as far south as Texas, but they caused wide fluctuations in sea level. When vast quantities of water were tied up in ice sheets, the sea level was three hundred to four hundred and fifty feet lower than at present, reaching its modern position only a few thousand years ago. The coastal features we know today—beaches, bays, and barrier islands—have formed since then.

Rivers bringing the sediment have moved back and forth, and some have skipped to new channels. Where the sands reach the sea they are carried along the coast by wave action and deposited, building a protective string of barrier islands like

Galveston Island. Bays are formed where river channels have been "drowned" behind the barrier islands, creating estuaries. In addition to the modern landscape, these geological processes have left a record of ancient river channels and former bays and barrier islands. Hurricanes and tropical storms are like exclamation marks in the development of coastal features, sometimes sharply accelerating the erosion or deposition.

So, in the end, we perch upon a great bowl of sediment, ten miles thick, with one edge at Austin and the other way out on the continental shelf, paralleling the coastline and stretching from Florida to the south of Mexico. The sediments tilt or dip gently toward the southeast, like a mushed layer cake.

But there is more: the sediments bore an organic load. All the vegetation incorporated and deposited with them—particularly in ancient lagoons much like the bays behind the barrier islands we know today—would decompose to become sources of oil and gas. And the oil and gas would creep upward along the dip slopes, and some would be trapped by geological features deriving from other kinds of movement. For one thing, the immense volumes of sediment eroding off the continental mass over the eons and being deposited as an advancing shoreline could not be endlessly accommodated without adjustments. The adjustments take the form of faults, or breaks, paralleling the coast. A good deal of oil and gas has been found by looking for faults and the traps they have formed, blocking oil and gas from migrating farther up the dip slopes.

A second kind of trap involves the geological phenomenon of rising salt. A thin but extensive layer of salt was deposited at a time when ocean circulation into the Gulf of Mexico was severely limited. Salt is lighter than the sediments. Over geological time, as breaks in the layer cake allowed the salt to start upward, pinnacles or domes of salt

moved through the sediments, sweeping up the overlying layers and trapping migrating oil and gas against the domes and along associated faults. Where these salt domes have come close to the surface, as at High Island, they have pushed the surface up into bumps of positive topography—icing on the cake, so to speak. Rising salt domes typically pushed up a cap; water circulating through this caprock and the bacteria found there combined in places to produce sulfur deposits. The domes at Boling and Moss Bluff in the Columbia Bottomlands were once sites of sulfur mining that fed Houston industry.

Other kinds of modest uplands in the region are relics of deposition, which are often identifiable by their vegetation. Pines like sandy soil, and the pines of Hermann Park, Memorial Park and the Sam Houston National Forest are there because of preserved sandy meanders and shorelines. The underlying sands and clays that dominate the soils likewise control the distribution of pines and other trees in the forests to the north of Houston. Coming southward into the city along Interstate 45, you go up a series of rises and down the gentler dip slopes. These bands of small hills also parallel the coast and represent sediments somewhat more resistant to erosion than the rest. Farther south, most rises in the prairie are remnants of the natural levees that formed around ancient stream meanders.

Water as an active agent at the surface has thus been a key to the evolution of the Houston Wilderness landscape. The bowl of sediment is also the reservoir for a great store of groundwater. Fresh water enters the sandy layers of the recharge zone to the north and west and it makes its way south in the Chicot and Evangeline aquifers. Water well turbines seen along Houston's Southwest Freeway, for example, tap groundwater at depths ranging from a few hundred to almost two thousand feet. Plentiful and cheap groundwater was an important resource for local agriculture, industry and development for almost a century, but it has been overproduced. From Houston's beginning through the 1980s, water levels in the wells dropped hundreds of feet.

What happens when the water is removed? The decrease in pressure results in irreversible compaction of some of the sediments. The clays in the aquifer layers were squashed, resulting in subsidence. The subsidence bowl centered along the Houston Ship Channel, which was the center of ambitious groundwater production. The ground level dropped about a foot for every hundred feet of water level decline, with a maximum ranging to

more than ten feet of subsidence in places. Lowering the surface in areas that were only a little above sea level to start with was a sure recipe for frequent and widespread flooding. Baytown's former Brownwood subdivision is a dramatic example of the toll taken by subsidence. Today a wetland park marks its return to wildness; its perimeter road is on the dike that was built in a doomed effort to protect the sinking waterfront development. Subsidence districts control groundwater pumping now, and Baytown relies instead on surface water supplies.

The region's landscape features may be subtle in elevation changes and understated in appearance, but there is no arguing with the force of the dynamic geological processes still at work.

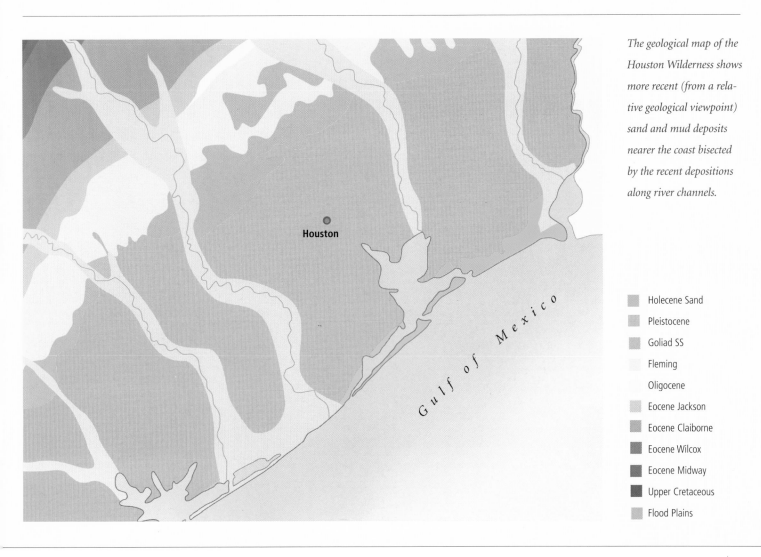

*The geological map of the Houston Wilderness shows more recent (from a relative geological viewpoint) sand and mud deposits nearer the coast bisected by the recent depositions along river channels.*

Houston

Gulf of Mexico

Holecene Sand

Pleistocene

Goliad SS

Fleming

Oligocene

Eocene Jackson

Eocene Claiborne

Eocene Wilcox

Eocene Midway

Upper Cretaceous

Flood Plains

# People on the Land

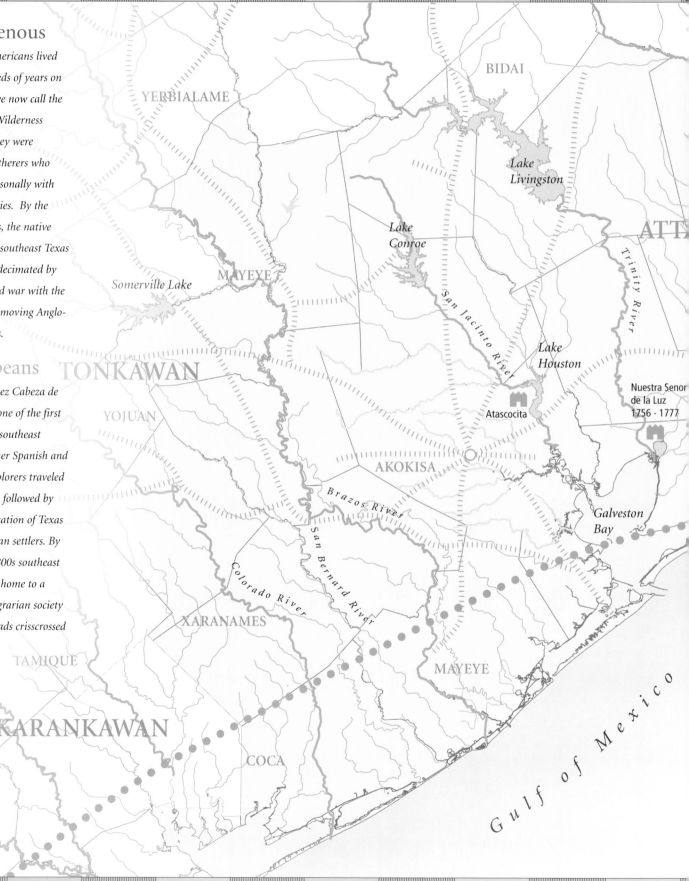

## Indigenous

*Native Americans lived for hundreds of years on the land we now call the Houston Wilderness region. They were hunter-gatherers who moved seasonally with food supplies. By the mid-1830s, the native peoples of southeast Texas had been decimated by disease and war with the westward-moving Anglo-Americans.*

## Europeans

*Alvar Nunez Cabeza de Vaca was one of the first to explore southeast Texas. Other Spanish and French explorers traveled the region, followed by the colonization of Texas by American settlers. By the late-1800s southeast Texas was home to a thriving agrarian society and railroads crisscrossed the region.*

BIDAI

YERBIALAME

Lake Livingston

Lake Conroe

Somerville Lake

MAYEYE

ATT

Trinity River

San Jacinto River

Lake Houston

TONKAWAN

Nuestra Senor de la Luz
1756 - 1777

YOJUAN

Atascocita

AKOKISA

Brazos River

Galveston Bay

San Bernard River

Colorado River

XARANAMES

TAMIQUE

MAYEYE

KARANKAWAN

COCA

Gulf of Mexico

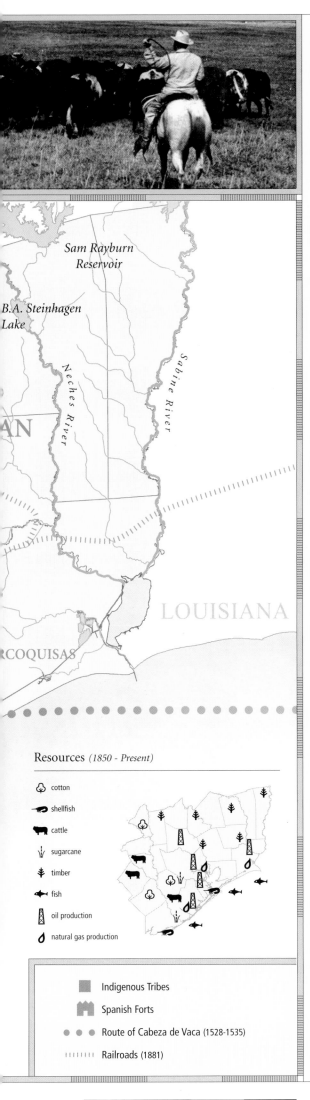

Sam Rayburn
Reservoir

B.A. Steinhagen
Lake

Neches River

Sabine River

LOUISIANA

COQUISAS

**Resources** *(1850 - Present)*

⚜ cotton

🦐 shellfish

🐄 cattle

🌾 sugarcane

🌲 timber

🐟 fish

▯ oil production

◊ natural gas production

▮ Indigenous Tribes

🏰 Spanish Forts

●●● Route of Cabeza de Vaca (1528-1535)

ııııııı Railroads (1881)

**THE HOUSTON WILDERNESS AREA** has been home for thousands of years to humans, who have impacted the land in a variety of ways. Our first glimpse of a human presence in southeast Texas is from the final millennia of the Late Wisconsin glaciations, some ten thousand years ago. Prevailing climatic conditions provided for a cooler, more humid environment than at present, with little seasonal change and frequent heavy rainfall. It was the age of the great mammals, or megafauna, and deciduous woodlands extended to the continental shelf. The habitat was perfect for the ancient megafauna of mammoths, mastodons, horses, camels, bison, dire wolves, saber-toothed cats, sloth, giant tortoise, armadillos, glyptodonts and capybara.

### The First People

People of the Late Paleo-Indian period, 10,000–7,000 years before the present (BP), were already living in the region as the great geologic and climatic transitions of the end of the glacial period occurred and the climate grew drier with more variation in the seasons. Prairies spread inland, and the mega fauna that had roamed the land during the Pleistocene (from 1.8 million to 10,000 years ago) became extinct during the Holocene (after 10,000 BP). Evidence of these

*Top of page: the early Spanish explorer, Alvar Nunez Cabeza de Vaca. Above: the American bison, Bison bison, commonly called the buffalo.*

0    2.5    5        10        15        20 miles

*The Akokisa Indian Village at Jesse H. Jones Park and Nature Center has reconstructed Akokisa huts to show visitors what life was like for these early residents of southeast Texas.*

animals and the people who hunted them in the Paleo-Indian period was discovered in dredged material from the floor of Galveston Bay and offshore Gulf sites.

With the climate changes of the Middle Holocene came hotter and drier weather. Rivers and streams dried up intermittently and prairie habitat expanded. Galveston Bay was formed when a river delta was drowned and people made their seasonal camps in the riparian woodlands on the banks of rivers, bayous and creeks that fed the bay. Archeologists investigating the Addicks Reservoir site in western Harris County found artifacts of the people who lived there during the period known as the Early Archaic (7,000–5,000 BP). In the Clear Lake watershed south of Houston, archeologists working at the Harris County Boys School excavation discovered a site occupied by people in the Middle Archaic period (5,000–3,500 BP). This site revealed a long human occupation beginning about 3,700 years ago, when the first shell middens appeared as the Galveston Bay system was established and the coast approached its present configuration. The site continued to be occupied seasonally until about 500 years ago, reaching into the time of recorded history.

Most of the local archeological information comes from the last three prehistoric periods— Late Archaic (3,500 BP), Early Ceramic (1,900–1,400 BP), and Late Prehistoric (1,400–500 BP). Hundreds of sites from these eras have been documented in the Houston Wilderness region. Numerous groups of people were using the local resources. The historic Indian period since 500 years ago has yielded few archeological sites, but by this stage the first historical record provided by European explorers had begun to give us a sense of how native peoples lived and interacted with one another and with the new arrivals.

Two Europeans stranded on the southeast Texas

coast have given us the most complete information about these early nomadic tribes. The first, Alvar Nuñez Cabeza de Vaca, was a member of the Spanish Narvaez expedition. He and some companions were shipwrecked off the upper Texas coast in 1528, probably on or near Galveston Island. They encountered two Native American groups from different tribes, the Copoque, a Karankawan tribe, and the Han, an Akokisan tribe. These people lived on the barrier islands from October to the end of February, depending largely on Rangia clams and oysters as a source of food. They built willow-ribbed living structures covered with mats and skins on the accumulated mounds of discarded clamshells. During the spring and summer they moved to inland camps on the shores of rivers and creeks. Here they gathered berries and other edibles and hunted mammals with bows and arrows.

De Vaca survived to live and travel with a series of native tribes, before reconnecting with Spanish soldiers in western Mexico in 1536. His account of the experience and the tribes he met, Cabeza de Vaca's Adventures in the Unknown Interior of America, makes vivid and absorbing reading. The next European to arrive was the French officer François Simars de Bellisle, who found himself marooned in Galveston Bay and was captured by a group of Akokisa in 1719. He lived with them as a captive until his rescue in 1721. They too were a migratory group, moving seasonally in a constant search for food. He saw no practice of horticulture. When Spanish government and church officials secured the southeastern borders of Texas against French traders in the mid-1700s, they recorded the major tribes and their territories. The predominant tribe was the Akokisa (or Orcoquisac), an Atakapa-speaking people ancestrally related to the Atakapa tribes to the east in Louisiana and friendly with the Bidai tribe, whose territory overlapped

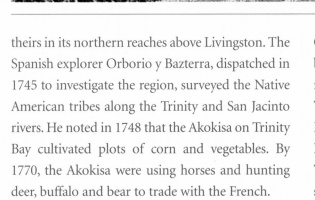

*Left: Sugarcane, Saccharum officinarum, being harvested. Sugarcane was one of the early crops cultivated in the Houston Wilderness region.*

theirs in its northern reaches above Livingston. The Spanish explorer Orborio y Bazterra, dispatched in 1745 to investigate the region, surveyed the Native American tribes along the Trinity and San Jacinto rivers. He noted in 1748 that the Akokisa on Trinity Bay cultivated plots of corn and vegetables. By 1770, the Akokisa were using horses and hunting deer, buffalo and bear to trade with the French.

Coco and Cujane people lived west of Galveston Bay. They were nomadic coastal tribes related to the Karankawa and seldom left the coastal areas. Tonkawa bands originally from territories north of Texas migrated to the prairies west of the Akokisa territory to escape attack from the Apaches.

The Akokisa, Atakapa, Bidai, Coco, Karankawa, and Tonkawa tribes were all hunter-gatherers who moved seasonally with food supplies; some have been reported to have practiced ritualistic cannibalism on captured enemies. Caddo people lived to the north and east of the Akokisa and Atakapa. They were woodland tribes with well-developed agricultural methods and a complex and sophisticated social structure; the Caddoan were considered more civilized by European standards.

Within a few decades of Bazterra's survey, however, the arrival of Europeans and Americans would forever change the lives and territories of these native peoples. By the mid-1830s, the native peoples of southeast Texas had been decimated by disease and war with the westward-moving Anglo-Americans. Only scattered camps remained, made up of occupants from several different tribes.

## Arrival of Europeans

The movement of Europeans into southeast Texas was a gradual process. There would be a long hiatus after Cabeza de Vaca's shipwreck. Spain claimed the territory but showed little interest in it until the French moved into Louisiana.

With the founding of the French port of New Orleans in 1718 came the need for trade goods to be shipped back to Europe. French traders began making their way across the Spanish border into Texas to trade with the native tribes. Joseph Blancpain, a Frenchman headquartered west of New Orleans, undertook regular trips into the Trinity River territory. By 1730, known routes into southeast Texas had been established. The intrusion into Spanish territory by the French was what motivated the Spanish to send Captain Bazterra to investigate the region, and he confirmed the French presence there. By 1754, Blancpain and his men had established a trading post and fort near the Trinity. Spain immediately countered the French encroachment and moved to secure the border by establishing the Mission Nuestra Señora de la Luz and the presidio of San Augustín de Ahumada del Orcoquisac on the lower Trinity River in 1756.

In 1762, King Louis XV of France gifted Louisiana to his cousin, Charles III, king of Spain. At the end of the Indian War or Seven Years' War, France lost most of her New World possessions. The Treaty of Paris signed in 1763 confirmed the transfer of Louisiana to Spain. Spain no longer had to protect the Louisiana-Texas border, and the mission and presidio on the lower Trinity were abandoned in 1771.

During the American Revolution, Spain would collaborate with her old enemy France to help the American colonists win independence from England. This temporary truce soon ended, however, and in 1800 Napoleon confiscated the Louisiana Territory from Spain with the Second Treaty of the San Ildefonso. In 1803, the United States purchased Louisiana from France. President Thomas Jefferson disputed the southern limit of Louisiana. He believed that the border was the Rio Grande and determined that the lands of Texas belonged to the United States. Again, Spain faced the need to secure the border in southeast Texas. In

*French privateer Jean Lafitte briefly governed a camp of settlers on Galveston Island, called Campeche, during the struggle for control of Texas lands between Spain and France.*

*Above: A reproduction of an early Texas plantation kitchen.*

*Stephen F. Austin was the first empresario, or colonizer, to bring settlers into southeast Texas, which was then a part of the newly independent government of Mexico.*

1805, Atascosito was established as a temporary mission near the old mission and presidio site on the lower Trinity River.

General James Wilkinson, commander of U.S. forces in Louisiana, proposed a compromise in 1806 for the border dispute with Spain. He offered to move his troops to the east of the Rio Hondo if the Spanish forces pulled back to the west of the Sabine River. Spanish Governor Simon de Herrera agreed to the proposal, resulting in the Neutral Ground Agreement. The agreed neutral ground soon became a lawless stretch of land between Texas and Louisiana. To prevent the outlaws from moving outside the neutral ground, Atascosito became a Spanish military post in 1812.

During this period, unrest erupted in Mexico against the Spanish government, and American filibusters joined with Mexican revolutionists to take control of Texas. One of the Mexican revolutionists, José Manuel Herra, created a government on Galveston Island and claimed it as part of the Mexican Republic. He appointed Louis Meshel Aury as governor. Henry Perry and Francisco Xavier Mina joined them. Their unsuccessful expedition ended the revolutionary stronghold on Galveston Island, and privateer Jean Lafitte took over the Aury camp. Lafitte called his camp Campeche. The exiled French general Charles Lellemand came to Lafitte's camp in 1818 to seek assistance in the last gasp of French encroachment into Spanish Texas. Lafitte helped Lellemand transport a group of French exiles up the Trinity River, where they established the short-lived colony called Le Champ d'Asile.

From the first Spanish excursion into southeast Texas in 1528 until the Louisiana Purchase in 1803, the Native American populations were considered a resource for European trade. Although infectious European diseases wrought havoc among local tribes, they were otherwise generally able to con-

duct their lives much as they had for centuries within their territories. Trade with the Europeans did bring some territorial change, as neighboring tribes moved closer to the trade routes and began to encroach on the historic Akokisa and Bidai lands. Karankawa and Coco bands moved to the western shore of Galveston Bay, and the Alabama and Coushatta moved into the southeast Texas areas that had once been home to the Caddo.

The Transcontinental Treaty in 1819 defined the western boundary of the Louisiana Purchase, ending the dispute over the neutral ground. This treaty set the stage for Anglo-American migration into Texas. The pioneers brought with them an insatiable appetite for land and natural resources that would forever alter both the lives of the Native American people and the natural landscapes of southeast Texas.

### The Sequence of Resource Extraction

After the American Revolution, Anglo-Americans were the first groups to move to new territories. They were settled in Mississippi and Louisiana by the 1780s, having traveled down the Mississippi River. When the United States finalized the Louisiana Purchase in 1803, groups of these restless Anglo-Americans were waiting at the Louisiana-Texas border. Many were stockmen, and in 1819, they had herds of branded cattle located on both sides of the Sabine River. By 1821 they were migrating into the areas that are now Chambers, Galveston, Harris, Jasper, Jefferson, and Liberty counties.

During that same period, American businessmen who had lost most of their assets during the last financial panic began looking at Texas as a place to recoup their losses. Moses Austin of Kentucky was the first to meet with the Spanish government leaders in Mexico. He convinced them that American immigration could help them develop Texas. Before he could fulfill his contract to bring in three hundred settlers, he died, and Mexico won

Left: Spindeltop Hill, near modern-day Beaumont, had over 285 active oil wells in 1902; only one year after oil was first discovered there.

its independence from Spain. It would be left to his son, Stephen F. Austin, to convince the new Mexican government that American immigration would be an asset to the Texas territory. Austin was the first empresario, or colonizer, in southeast Texas. He was followed by Vehlein, Zavala, Burnett and Robertson.

Immigration was not limited to southern Anglo-Americans. Advertisements and letters went to many foreign countries. Men from twenty-four American states and eleven different countries fought at the Battle of San Jacinto in 1836, when Texas was wrested from Mexican rule to become a republic. African Americans and Native Americans were also among those who in time formed the population of the tiny settlement of Houston, then called Harrisburg.

The new settlers were lured by a cornucopia of resources and opportunity. Thousands of acres of untouched fertile land, miles of tallgrass prairies, an abundance of fresh water, rich forests of virgin timber and tens of thousands of wild horses and longhorn cattle awaited the new arrivals. Galveston Bay provided several port sites and was fed on all sides by navigable rivers and bayous. The rich estuarine waters promised unlimited fisheries. By the 1840s Galveston had a population of four thousand, and Houston had expanded to some twenty-four hundred residents by the 1850 census. Settlers constantly pushed into tribal territories, and fighting continued between immigrants and Native Americans.

Southeast Texas was an agrarian society, self-sufficient and economically independent, by the time of the fledgling republic's annexation to the United States in 1846. During the early days of statehood the agricultural wealth grew. Cotton, cattle, and sugar fed the economy. Shipping by water was the only transportation method. A canal was dredged to connect the lower Brazos River to the Galveston Channel. The canal made it easier to ship cotton and sugar from the large plantations located between the Brazos and Colorado rivers. Herds of

cattle from the coastal saltgrass prairies were delivered to the New Orleans market by trail drives or shipped in small lots from Galveston, Houston and Beaumont. A rail line was chartered, and in 1859 the Galveston, Houston and Henderson Railroad line was completed from Galveston to Houston.

Virgin stands of cypress, oak, cedar, mulberry, ash and pine timber were cut from the riparian corridors of the Sabine, Neches, Trinity and San Jacinto rivers and their many tributaries. The logs were pulled to the water's edge by teams of oxen, rolled into the water, and rafted down the waterways to lumber mills built near the bays. The lumber was then shipped to the East Coast and European markets. By now, the indigenous population was so depleted by disease and conflict with settlers that Native Americans had all but vanished from the region.

The Civil War devastated the cotton and sugar-based economy, which depended heavily upon slaves. From 1865 to 1880, cattle would be the resource that brought Texas financial stability. In the years from 1870 through the 1890s rail lines sprang up across the region. Smaller holdings replaced large plantations, and agriculture grew to include produce farms. Cattle shared the land with rice fields as fencing began to chop up the open range. Railroads helped to change the forested landscape as lumber barons moved their mills into previously unreachable areas of the Big Thicket. At the turn of the twentieth century, the next great resource boom set in. Oil became king after Spindletop began gushing its wealth into the Beaumont area. Soon oil derricks punctuated the southeast Texas landscape. Oil brought refineries and industry to the area, and development exploded across the region.

The history of southeast Texas clearly illustrates how resource-rich it is. The land that nurtured native peoples for thousands of years has gone on to make modern fortunes.

Above: Slave shackles. The Civil War devastated Texas' cotton and sugar-based economy, which depended heavily on slaves.

On Jan. 10, 1901 the Lucas Gusher blew in, beginning the oil boom at Spindeltop Hill in southeast Texas.

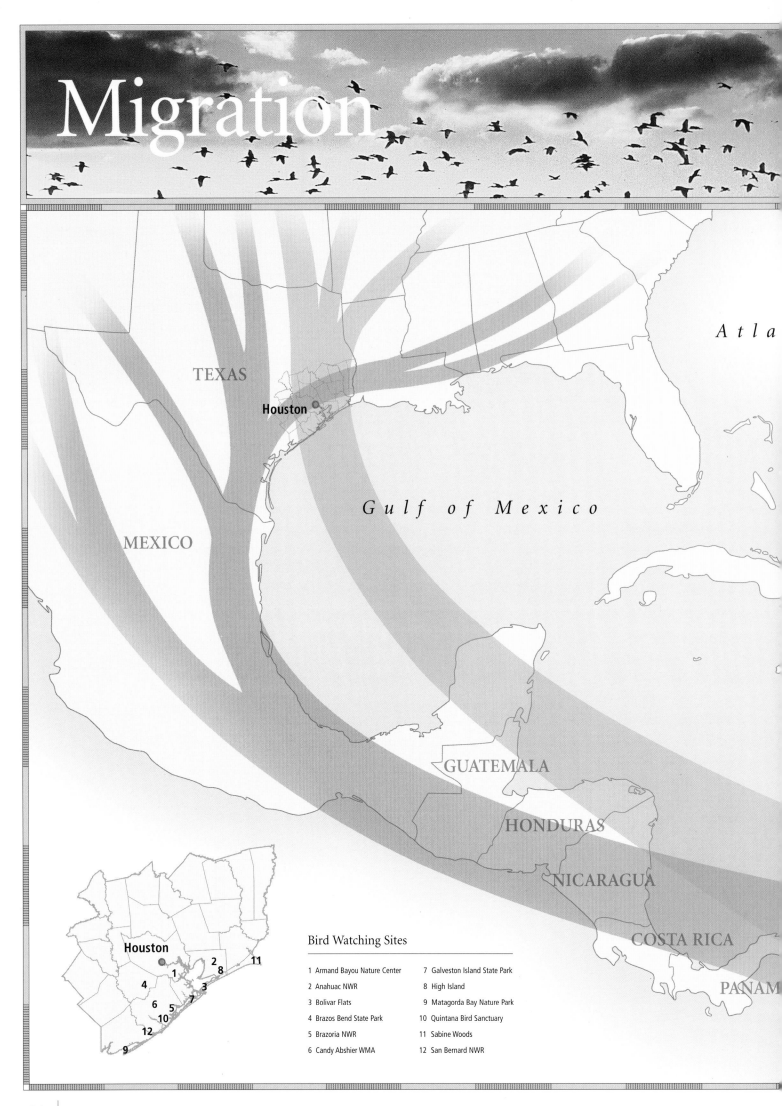

# Migration

TEXAS

Houston

MEXICO

Gulf of Mexico

Atla

PANAM

GUATEMALA

HONDURAS

NICARAGUA

COSTA RICA

PANAM

Houston

## Bird Watching Sites

| | |
|---|---|
| 1 Armand Bayou Nature Center | 7 Galveston Island State Park |
| 2 Anahuac NWR | 8 High Island |
| 3 Bolivar Flats | 9 Matagorda Bay Nature Park |
| 4 Brazos Bend State Park | 10 Quintana Bird Sanctuary |
| 5 Brazoria NWR | 11 Sabine Woods |
| 6 Candy Abshier WMA | 12 San Bernard NWR |

*Ocean*

*Caribbean Sea*

VENEZUELA

COLOMBIA

Land Birds and Birds of Prey

Shore Birds and Wading Birds

**BATS, FISH, MOTHS,** crabs, dragonflies, butterflies and birds: they all migrate. The phenomenon is more widespread than we usually suppose. Our Houston region is a focal point in the great bird migrations in North America, whose scope and complexity is only generally understood. Some visitors are so large and arrive in such noticeable numbers that they become harbingers of the fall. When groups of tall gray sandhill cranes cruise in to land on the west end of Galveston Island, or flights of glittering white snow geese invade the Katy Prairie by the tens of thousands, even the uninitiated can sense the power and beauty of migration.

But these large, charismatic birds are far from being the only migrants that depend on the Houston Wilderness. The Houston Audubon Society's Bolivar Flats Shorebird Sanctuary shelters and feeds hundreds of thousands of migrating shorebirds, a record unmatched by any other spot on the Texas coast. The flats were created by the building in 1898 of the five-mile-long north jetty to protect the mouth of Galveston Bay. Sand piled up behind the jetty, creating the flats, which are heavily visited by migrants such as sanderlings, sandpipers, godwits and other shorebirds, some arriving as early as July and pausing to build up energy reserves for a journey as far south as Tierra del Fuego.

*Because of the sheer number of birds that migrate through southeast Texas, the Houston Wilderness region has excellent bird-watching opportunities.*

0    2.5    5    10    15    20 miles

While the shorebirds are easily seen feeding and loafing on the flats, another impressive migration is going on overhead. Every fall, broad-winged and Swainson's hawks from all over northeastern North America funnel down the Texas coast, soaring thousands of feet high on the warming air, slowly advancing south in spiraling, energy-saving formations called kettles. As they edge along Galveston Bay, the kettles may include thousands of birds. When Hurricane Rita struck the upper Texas coast in 2005, the hawks hitched a ride on the northerly winds sweeping down the storm's western edge, soaring over Smith Point on Trinity Bay, headed for South America. Only in the last fifteen years or so has this spectacle been closely scrutinized. Now our region participates in the international Hawkwatch program. Teams of professionals and volunteers spend September and October identifying and counting the hawks from a platform at Candy Abshier Wildlife Management Area, one of a dozen Galveston Bay sites that the Gulf Coast Bird Observatory uses to study migration.

Migrating neotropical song birds—the warblers, buntings, orioles, flycatchers and others—use the upper Texas coast as a stopover on their way north as well as south. Birdwatchers from all over the world come to see the spring migration, and no spot is better known among them than the Houston Audubon Society's sanctuaries in the town of High Island. Situated at the neck of the Bolivar Peninsula, High Island is not so much an island as a high spot created by an underground salt dome. Thickly wooded with coastal live oaks and other native trees, High Island offers the first forested sanctuary that neotropical birds see after flying five hundred to six hundred miles across the Gulf of Mexico from the Yucatan Peninsula (see the Columbia Bottomlands chapter for more about the rigors of migration and the importance of stopover habitats).

Beginning in April and running through the end of May, swarms of birds wait for a prevailing south-easterly wind. When it comes, they take what seems a great leap of faith, launching themselves into the night to fly across the Gulf. Their routes vary with the winds, and typically they arrive in Texas by mid-morning. They rest and feed and move on, pressed by the urgent need to head north to breeding grounds and find the best nesting sites and mates.

Day-traveling birds such as hawks, cranes and waterfowl navigate by visual landmarks, sometimes following older birds that have learned the routes from their parents. But the night-flying neotropicals have no landmarks. Scientists have created elaborate experiments to try to understand how birds know how and when to migrate. By releasing birds in a planetarium, they have determined that some species can orient themselves by the stars. Others seem able to orient themselves to the north, possibly with the aid of miniscule magnetic deposits in their bodies. The decision to launch seems to be timed to the lengthening day, and birds seem subtly aware of changes in atmospheric conditions.

To prepare themselves for the flight, neotropicals gorge on insects, larding themselves with fat deposits. A warbler weighing half an ounce, or about fifteen grams, can add six to seven grams of fat and burns up a gram every hundred and twenty-five miles. For a six-hundred-mile flight, that does not leave much of a margin of error. If all goes well, the bird's own flying speed of eighteen to twenty-five miles an hour is amplified by a tail wind of fifteen to forty miles an hour. Many birds attain average speeds of fifty miles an hour and can easily reach the Texas coast and keep on cruising to inland forests.

But if the birds encounter a sudden spring norther over the middle of the Gulf, the result can be a disaster, with tens of thousands of bright-colored bodies dumped into the water. Those that do survive create a "fallout" in which exhausted birds crowd into the

nearest coastal trees to rest and feed. During a fallout dozens of species can be seen. High Island is one such place, justly celebrated and visited by birders from far and wide. The Texas coast is dotted with small wooded areas that serve as "migrant traps," where even a few trees on a few acres can provide an invaluable place to shelter and recover.

Another such locale is the Quintana Bird Sanctuary system, ten miles south of Lake Jackson on the man-made island of Quintana. Consisting of only four acres in six city lots but strategically close to the Gulf shore, the sanctuary has been planted with native toothache trees and other woody flowering natives and enhanced with watering sites. It is not unusual to get close views of warblers, orioles, buntings and grosbeaks there.

While the spring migration reaching the Texas coast over the water may seem riskier than the fall migration over the land, two-thirds of migration losses occur during the fall, as young birds with no mother to guide them make their way down the coast. The fall migration is less concentrated and dramatic than that of spring but no less important. At the grounds of the Gulf Coast Bird Observatory (GBCO) on Buffalo Camp Bayou in the city of Lake Jackson, bird feeders and butterfly and hummingbird gardens draw other migrants as well. Many Houstonians are accustomed to seeing migrant ruby-throated hummingbirds arriving in the spring from their migration across the Gulf. The tiny birds pass through town again in the fall on their way down the coast, crowding feeders, and then most are gone. During the winter though, the GCBO feeders and flowering plants draw five different species of hummingbirds—ruby-throated, Anna's, black-chinned, buff-bellied and rufous. These are what are called temperate migrants, fleeing the mountains of the western states for the winter.

As noted, birds are not the only migrants. Members of the colony of Mexican free-tailed bats that live under the Waugh Street bridge over Buffalo Bayou in Houston are likely to have migrated from Mexico. The black witch moth, sometimes mistaken for a bat because of its large wing size—up to seven inches in span—also migrates from Mexico. Triggered by the beginning of the rainy season in Mexico, in June and July the black witches move north, traveling at night like other moths, appearing under the eaves of buildings and sometimes entering rooms. Little, if anything, is known about their southward migration. But they are stubborn and persistent fliers. Some have been seen swept up in hurricanes in Mexico and blown to the Texas coast.

Perhaps the most famous migrant is the monarch butterfly. The monarchs' migration to a densely wooded, remote Mexican valley is widely known. So many monarchs congregate there that they bend the branches of trees, yet these migrants have never been to this spot before. The instinct to migrate appears to be genetically encoded in the butterflies and passed on from generation to generation, another example of the wonder of migration. Perhaps the monarchs that grow from caterpillars on milkweed in Texas may be the ones to complete the trip deep into Mexico—who knows? Our location on the flight path of all these cosmopolitan long-distance travelers connects us closely with life far to the north and south. To complete their taxing journeys every year, the birds and bats and butterflies depend on our effective stewardship of our natural assets.

### Bird Watching Sites

*Armand Bayou Nature Center, Anahuac NWR, Bolivar Flats, Brazos Bend State Park, Brazoria NWR, Candy Abshier WMA, Galveston Island State Park, High Island, Matagorda Bay Nature Park, Quintana Bird Sanctuary, Sabine Woods, San Bernard NWR*

# Ecoregion Overview

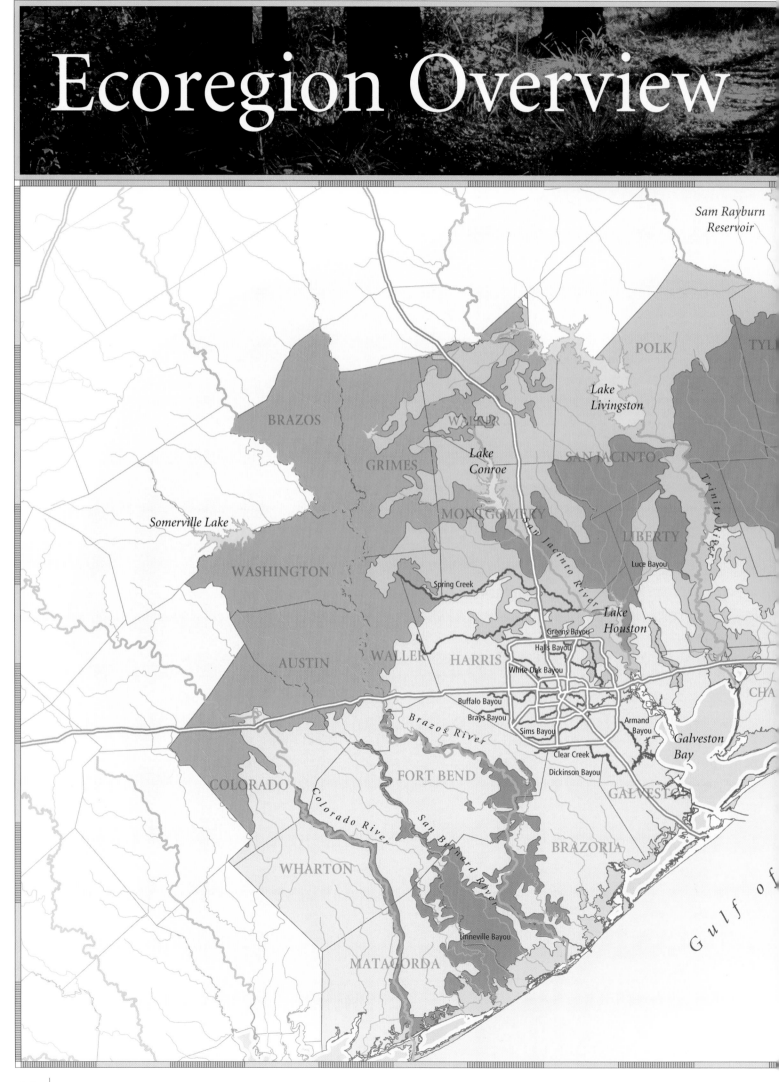

Sam Rayburn
Reservoir

POLK

TYL

Lake
Livingston

BRAZOS

WALKER

Lake
Conroe

GRIMES

SAN JACINTO

Trinity River

Somerville Lake

MONTGOMERY

LIBERTY

San Jacinto River

Luce Bayou

WASHINGTON

Spring Creek

Lake
Houston

Greens Bayou

WALLER

Halls Bayou

AUSTIN

HARRIS

White Oak Bayou

CHA

Buffalo Bayou

Brays Bayou

Brazos River

Armand
Bayou

Galveston
Bay

Sims Bayou

COLORADO

Clear Creek

FORT BEND

Dickinson Bayou

GALVESTO

Colorado River

San Bernard River

BRAZORIA

WHARTON

Linneville Bayou

Gulf of

MATAGORDA

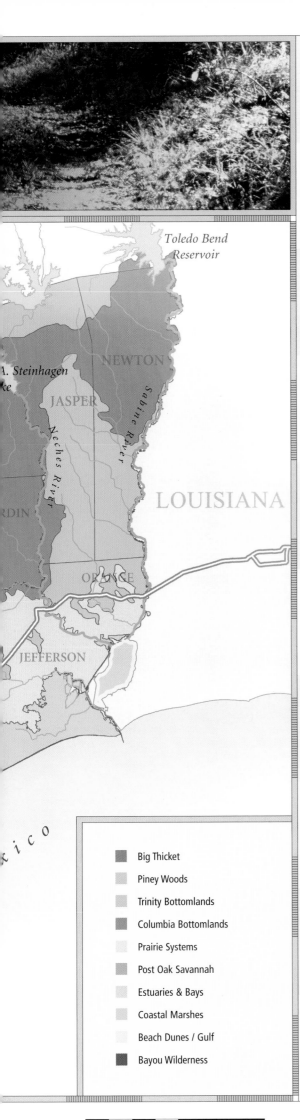

**BIG THICKET** *To the northeast is the fabled Big Thicket, an area of ecological convergence that is unrivaled in its diversity of plant life. Within the Big Thicket are found eleven distinct ecological systems, varying from stands of longleaf pine to bogs populated by carnivorous plants.*

**PINEY WOODS** *This area of rolling topography and sandier soils is laced with numerous creeks and smaller rivers with their clear water, sand bars, and localized strips of hardwoods. The pine forests are home to a multitude of plant and animal species, including the endangered red-cockaded woodpecker.*

**TRINITY BOTTOMLANDS** *To the northeast lies the Trinity River and its wide, forested bottomlands. This area is relatively undeveloped and contains extensive swamps and backwaters. Here one finds water-loving cypress and tupelo trees, along with the yellow prothonotary warbler.*

**COLUMBIA BOTTOMLANDS** *A double-canopy forest called the Columbia Bottomlands grows in the fertile floodplains of three river systems that flow into the Gulf of Mexico-the Colorado, San Bernard and the Brazos. These bottomlands are distinguished for their use by migrating neotropical bird species in the spring.*

**PRAIRIE SYSTEMS** *Originally most of the coastal prairies in the area were covered with tall grass and dotted with pothole wetlands. A large portion of this prairie has been converted to farmland or managed grazing, but still functions as a sponge for the region, soaking up rainfall and sheltering a variety of wildlife.*

**POST OAK SAVANNAH** *To the northwest, the prairie yields to the post oak savannah ecosystem. This zone is typified by rolling topography, and in its natural state is an open woodland of post oak trees underlain by grasslands. The savannah is characterized by abundant, beautiful wildflowers in the spring.*

**ESTUARIES & BAYS** *The Houston Wilderness area contains three great estuaries: Sabine Lake; the Galveston Bay system; and the Matagorda Bay system. These bays and estuaries are places where fresh water from rivers and salt water come together to create some of the most productive ecosystems anywhere on the globe.*

**COASTAL MARSHES** *The southern edge of the Houston Wilderness area is a fringe of coastal marshes that provide the transition zone between higher coastal prairies and the waters of our bays and estuaries. These marshlands are key habitats for wintering waterfowl—a national and international resource.*

**GULF OF MEXICO** *The barrier island beaches and dune systems separate the bays from the Gulf of Mexico, the largest of the ecological systems in the Houston Wilderness area. A tremendous variety of fish and marine mammals, birds and even coral reefs call the gulf home.*

**BAYOU WILDERNESS** *The bayous that wind their way through the city of Houston—a unique hybrid of urban wilderness—are ribbons of natural space that connect ecoregions and are important for flood control, wildlife habitat, recreational opportunities and their role in our cultural heritage.*

# Big Thicket

21

94

19

94

287

**Corrigan**

*Neches River*

*Sam Rayburn Reservoir*

63

69

287

*Lake Livingston*

**Woodville**

*Martin Dies*

*Beech Creek*

*Theuvenins Creek*

19

**Livingston**

190

*Sandy Creek*

*Hickory Creek*

*Turkey Creek*

**Huntsville**

30

156

*Lake Livingston SP*

*Menard Creek*

*Big Sandy Creek*

*Turkey Creek*

*Huntsville SP*

150

150

146

69

Roy E. Larsen
Sandyland Sa

Si

**Kountze**

*Trinity River*

*Cypress Creek*

787  Trinity River NWR

*Pine Island*

*Little Pine Island Bayou*

Lance Rosier

326

**Conroe**

105

Davis Hill SNA

306

105  **Batson**

*Bayou*

105

*San Jacinto River*

59

**The Woodlands**

45

*Lake Conroe*

105  146

**Sour Lake**

*Lake Houston SP*

Trinity River NWR

321

90  **Liberty**

365

**Spring**

249

1960

**Atascocita**

*Lake Houston*

Trinity River NWR

146

61

1406

8

## Map labels

Toledo Bend Reservoir

(255) (505) (63) (505)

sper

(190)

(389)

(96) (87) (109)

es Bottom / Gore B

*Sabine River*

(62) (12)

e Creek SP

mont

Tony Houseman WMA

(10)

Lower Neches WMA - Adams Bayou

Lower Neches WMA - Bessie Height

eaumont

5)

*Murphee undment*

### Legend

■ Big Thicket

■ State Parks, WMA's and National Wildlife Refuges, National Parks

0   3   6   12   18   24 miles

---

**THE EASTERN PORTION** of the Houston Wilderness features a great forest commonly known as the Big Thicket. Most of us have heard of the Big Thicket, but few have a firm handle on exactly where it is, and indeed opinions on the matter range widely.

For many, the Big Thicket is chiefly in the seven counties that today contain the Big Thicket National Preserve: Hardin, Tyler, Jasper, Polk, Liberty, Orange and Jefferson counties. Based on vegetation or soil characteristics, others contend that the Big Thicket also includes portions of several neighboring counties, ranging from Newton County on the Louisiana border to as far away as Montgomery or even Grimes counties. Using a culturally derived definition rather than biological or geological criteria, a number of local residents are adamant that the Big Thicket takes in only Hardin and southern Polk counties—the locations of the famous bear hunts of the early twentieth century.

Regardless of how it is defined, the Big Thicket is an ecological jewel. The Big Thicket National Preserve, covering almost 100,000 acres of the 3-million-acre area often described as the historic Big Thicket, was designated in 1981 as an International Biosphere Reserve and in 2001 as a Globally Important Bird Area. Village Creek and

*Hiking opportunities abound in the Big Thicket ecoregion less than two hours from the urban metropolis of Houston.*

Martin Dies Jr. State Park conserve additional portions of the Big Thicket and provide a wide range of camping and recreational opportunities. The 5,654-acre Roy E. Larsen Sandylands Sanctuary, managed by the Nature Conservancy, includes important longleaf pine habitat and endangered species. Whether one is a scientist, naturalist, hiker, birder, kayaker, canoeist, camper, hunter or angler, the Big Thicket has much to offer.

People often want to know what is so special about the Big Thicket and how it came about. Books describing the area and its cultural heritage include James Corzine's Saving the Big Thicket: From Exploration to Preservation, 1685–2003, Francis Abernethy's Tales of the Big Thicket, Campbell and Lynn Loughmiller's Big Thicket Legacy, and Pete Gunter's The Big Thicket: An Ecological Reevaluation (see Further Reading). The best way to answer what makes it special is to experience it, especially with someone who can interpret its more subtle features. But you don't need a guide to enjoy most aspects of the place.

It takes little specialized knowledge to absorb the sunshine on a brilliant blue afternoon, lazily drifting down Village Creek in a kayak, hearing only birds, frogs and the ripple of water as you lift your paddle from the creek. Thanks to land acquisitions by the Big Thicket National Preserve along Village Creek in 2005 (with the assistance of the Conservation Fund), this wonderful, relaxing experience, which includes large stretches of backcountry scenery, will be protected for generations to come. Further acquisitions are planned on the creek.

It takes even less preparation to enjoy hiking on the region's numerous and varied trails. Imagine setting out on the fifteen-mile Turkey Creek Trail of the Big Thicket National Preserve on a cool spring morning. You start off by gradually descending into the bottoms of Village Creek. Proceeding along a boardwalk that keeps hikers out of the mud, you enjoy a cool breeze and the sweet smell of the surrounding magnolia, beech and loblolly pine trees. The spring migration is intensifying: if you start early enough, you may spy numerous bird species, ranging from the bright red of a scarlet or summer tanager to the brilliant blue of an indigo bunting.

Woodpeckers are hammering away in the distance as you pass near numerous baygalls and cypress sloughs. Baygalls are depressions that hold water for portions of the year, and they generally feature distinct vegetation, such as gallberry holly, sweetbay, red bay, titi and blackgum. Some cypress sloughs have towering ancient cypress trees surrounded by "knees" emerging from the water and reaching six feet or more in height.

After crossing over the lush bank of Village Creek you begin an ascent up to one of the area's large sandhills. In dramatic contrast to the wetter environment of the bottoms, the sandhill is breezy and dry. Longleaf pines cast their thinner shade over cacti and yucca. Roadrunners may dart across the trail. If you were to walk the entire trail, the variety would continue, including upland longleaf pine forests and a savannah filled with flowers and carnivorous pitcher plants, one of four kinds of carnivorous plants found here.

To appreciate the Big Thicket fully, it helps to understand something of its natural and cultural history. It appears to be a product of a major contraction of the Gulf of Mexico, when the waters receded to approximately the modern shoreline. Left behind was an immense region that had been submerged for long ages. Over the subsequent thousands of years the terrain was altered by the erosion and deposition work of the great rivers of the region—the Trinity, Neches and Sabine—seeking their way to the Gulf.

What was created was a mosaic of subtle topography featuring an immense range of soils and

vegetation. The Big Thicket has greater variety of soil types than any area of comparable size in the nation. As a result, plants typical of regions as far away as Appalachia and the Ohio Valley are present—patches of the great aboriginal eastern forest of North America are within picnicking distance of Houston. And this is where east meets west: plants of drier western lands reach their easterly limits in the sandier parts of the Big Thicket, where abundant rainfall is rapidly wicked away and dry-country plants are the ones that do best. A forested patchwork with a bewildering diversity of plants emerged. Naturally occurring fires likely resulted in open, parklike uplands, with the network of rivers, creeks, bayous and sloughs offering densely forested conditions in the bottomlands.

For generations people have seen the Big Thicket as bountiful and have come to harvest its resources. Few Native Americans made it their permanent home, although numerous hunting camps and other sites of temporary use have been documented. Spanish and French expeditions entering East Texas in the sixteenth and seventeenth centuries encountered a great forest or monte grande, impenetrable in places and reaching up river valleys far to the north. The Spanish pattern of mission building and farming settlement reflected the challenging quality of the forest, as most activities occurred to the north, avoiding settlement in the heart of the Big Thicket. Not until the lumber boom of the nineteenth century would the forest begin to see permanent human occupation.

Today the Big Thicket has been dramatically transformed. Large portions of it have been converted to pine plantations, pastures, or residential, commercial or transportation uses. But remnants of its wildness persist, creating vignettes of what Native Americans and early explorers saw, and revealing even now an extraordinary variety of plant communities. Botanists may disagree over the number of

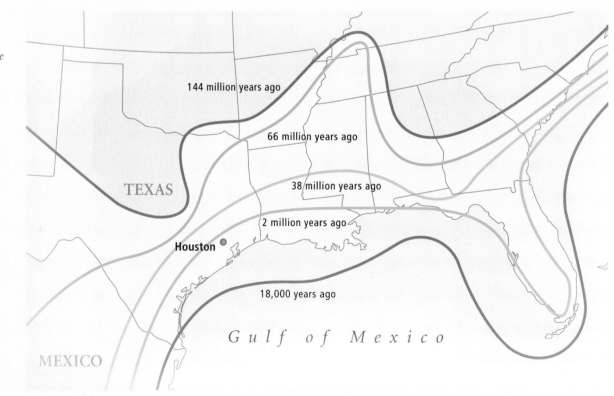

*The shoreline of the Gulf*
*coast has changed tremen-*
*dously several times over the*
*course of geological history.*
*The 18,000-year line shows*
*the shoreline when the sea*
*level was much lower than*
*it is today because of the*
*water that was tied up in*
*glacial ice sheets.*

distinct plant associations in the Big Thicket, but all of us can appreciate the extraordinary variety and richness of its upland forests, slope forests, flood-plain forests, flatland forests, prairies and baygalls.

## Upland Forests

*Pine Sandhill*—The driest of the forests in south-east Texas is the pine sandhill woodlands, occurring on deep sandy terrace deposits along creeks and rivers. The best examples in Big Thicket are at the Nature Conservancy's Roy E. Larsen Sandylands Sanctuary and in the southeast portion of the Turkey Creek unit of the national preserve. These are low, open woodlands (short forest) with a relatively sparse herbaceous layer and much exposed sand. There is a scattered overstory of lon-gleaf, loblolly and shortleaf pines; the understory is a layer of oaks, mainly bluejack and post oaks inter-laced with the occasional prickly pear and yucca.

*Pine Forest*—This kind of forest is widely distrib-uted throughout the Big Thicket and is found on well-drained uplands (see the Pineywoods chapter for more about this forest type). Examples of this association can be found in the northern area of the Big Sandy Creek unit of the national preserve and in Martin Dies Jr. State Park.

*Pine Savannah Wetland*—Savannahs occur in areas of poor drainage. Usually widely scattered longleaf pines are the only trees present, although stunted individual blackgum and sweetgum may be present. Midstory shrubs are sweetbay, wax myrtle, titi and gallberry holly. The herbaceous layer is diverse, including insectivorous species such as pitcher plants and sundews, and orchids are usually common. Sedges are also common, as is standing water.

Famed Big Thicket botanist Geraldine Watson has noted of this community, "Nowhere else in our region has the intricate relationship of plants to one another and to their environment achieved such an advanced and delicate balance."

The Sundew Trail in the Hickory Creek Savannah unit of the national preserve offers the best example of pine savannah wetland in the region. Since this plant community is now extremely rare throughout its original range, the national preserve is seeking to restore additional areas of pine savannah wetland in the newly acquired Village Creek Savannahs area of the Village Creek Corridor.

## Slope Forests

*Upper Slope Pine-Oak*—Among the associations known as slope forests (those growing on land sloping down toward rivers, streams and bayous), the upper slope pine-oak community is the driest. The dominant overstory species are shortleaf pine and red, post, or blackjack oaks, and loblolly pine is almost always present. Dominant shrubs are yaupon, flowering dogwood and beautyberry. The herbaceous layer is restricted because of the well-developed canopy. A good example of upper slope pine-oak forest is found at the start of the Kirby Nature Trail in the Turkey Creek unit of the national preserve.

*Mid-Slope Oak-Pine*—These woodlands feature a taller, more closed canopy and have a greater pro-portion of hardwoods in the overstory than in their upper slope counterparts. Overstory dominant species are red oak, white oak and loblolly pine. Dominant shrubs are flowering dogwood, American holly, and yaupon. A good example is found along the Kirby Nature Trail in the Turkey Creek unit of the national preserve as one approaches Village Creek.

*Lower Slope Hardwood-Pine*—Found on the gen-tle to steep slopes near creeks and creek branches, this association has a dense closed canopy and is dominated by beech, magnolia and loblolly pine. Sweetgum, blackgum and oaks are common in the understory along with other dominant species of

American holly, red maple, American hornbeam, horse sugar and yaupon. This association is encountered alongside Village Creek on the Kirby Nature Trail of the national preserve and in Village Creek State Park near Lumberton, Texas.

### Floodplain Forests

*Stream Floodplain*—In the bottoms along major creeks or streams on low, flat terrain that regularly floods grows the community called stream flood-plain forest. Beech and loblolly pine are dominant; water oak, basket oak, willow oak and laurel oak are typical; and magnolia is present. The understory is normally open with some small trees or iron-wood and American holly. The sparse herbaceous layer is dominated by grasses, sedges and cane. Leaf litter is largely absent due to winter flooding.

*River Floodplain*—On the broad flats of the Neches River floodplain and tributaries of Beech Creek and Pine Island Bayou is river floodplain forest. Tree growth is rapid, and many trees reach great size, which is accentuated by the open under-story. Shellbark hickory, and a variety of oaks—basket, cherrybark, overcup, willow and laurel—dominate the ovestory. Vines are more important here than in other woodland types and the ground surface is usually devoid of leaf litter.

*Cypress-Tupelo Swamp*—The deeper backwaters, sloughs, oxbows and depressions are where cypress and tupelo trees flourish. Both may reach immense proportions and form large buttresses. Edge species may be buttonbush, Carolina ash, water elm and water hickory. The Pine Island Bayou Corridor and the Jack Gore Baygall and Neches Bottomlands units of the national preserve offer excellent oppor-tunities to see this plant association.

### Flatland Forests

*Flatland Hardwood-Pine*—This type of woodland is restricted to the geological formation known as the Beaumont surface and, in the Big Thicket, is restricted to the Lance Rosier unit of the national preserve and some adjacent areas. The key to recognition is the absence of beech. Dominant tree species are white oak, southern red oak, magnolia, water oak and loblolly pine. The understory is dense with yaupon, American holly, horse sugar, and red bay. The herb layer is sparse.

*Flatland Hardwood*—In the same area is the flat-land hardwood community found in low ground along creek drainages. Laurel oak and blackgum are the principal species. Basket oak, sweetgum, water oak, cherrybark oak and willow oak are common. Shrubs include palmetto and arrow-wood. The preponderance of dense stands of large palmettos is a remarkable feature of this associa-tion, and may be unique to the Big Thicket.

### Prairies

*Mixed-Grass Prairie*—These nearly level, slowly drained plains are vegetated mostly with grassland but have a scattering of shrubs and trees through-out. Found today on uplands between the Trinity River and Pine Island Bayou, these prairies likely stem from soil types that resist root penetration and the downward percolation of water. Though little mixed-grass prairie was included within the bound-aries of the national preserve, the pristine twelve-acre Marysee prairie, north of State Highway 105 just outside Batson, has been saved by the Big Thicket Association, which owns and manages it.

### Baygalls

These may occur within most of the major plants asso-ciations described. Baygalls may from wherever water accumulates and stands for most of the year. Principal species are titi, gallberry holly, sweetbay, red bay and blackgum. Among the ferns common in baygalls are Christmas, cinnamon and royal ferns. Sphagnum, other mosses and liverworts are found as well.

## The Future of the Big Thicket

The Big Thicket has been a survivor. You can witness beautiful, serene sunrises on the Neches River as the fog slowly lifts. You can take a peaceful hike through quiet forests where the only sounds come from birds, insects and an occasional breeze rustling the leaves. Despite decades of timber harvests, conversion of native forest to plantations, oil and gas extraction, and increasing suburban and commercial development, the Big Thicket remains a place of wonder. Areas have been set aside to ensure that future generations can know its distinctive plant associations and enjoy their beauty.

The National Preserve is unusual though, as it is not a contiguous, cohesive area, but an accumulation of individual, smaller preserves. Fortunately, besides the Big Thicket National Preserve, Village Creek and Martin Dies Jr. state parks, and the Nature Conservancy's Roy E. Larsen Sandylands Sanctuary, a series of smaller preserves and parks managed by timber companies, land trusts, counties and cities all work together to save special places in the region. Even taken together, though, these parcels' total area is quite small relative to the overall Big Thicket, and their dispersed geography leaves them threatened as their surroundings change.

Until recently the preserves and parks were mostly surrounded by managed timberlands. With the decline of that industry in the area leading to the sale of over a million acres of land, the area is now far more subdivided and increasingly destined for subdivisions and commercial development rather than timber farming. Conserved areas find themselves next door to developed areas rather than managed timberlands. This development, unless unusually sensitively done, reduces and fragments wildlife habitat, allows exotic species to replace native plants and impairs water quality as a result of fertilizer and pesticide use and runoff from hardened surfaces. Natural viewsheds and soundscapes are replaced with the sights and sounds of suburbs and commerce. Preservation of our Big Thicket heritage in this changed environment will require purchasing more of the surrounding land, or facilitating conservation easements and other private land management plans to maintain a buffer zone.

New reservoirs perennially being discussed for the region's rivers also loom as a major threat to the Big Thicket. They would divert essential water from the floodplain forests and eliminate the periodic floods crucial to maintaining wet soil conditions and nutrient levels. Along with the elimination or reduction of floods to the floodplain forests, the timing of flows and even the quantity of water in the basin could change if water is shipped out to distant cities, as is currently proposed in some projects. Such projects could have significant effects on estuaries downstream as well as on the floodplain forests.

Fortunately, dealing responsibly with these threats is well within our power as our region increasingly appreciates the extraordinary resources and opportunities that the place represents. For example, black bears seem to be poised for a slow return. The Louisiana subspecies (Ursus americanus luteolus) that historically occurred in the area is federally listed as a threatened species. Restoration work in Louisiana, Arkansas and Oklahoma has already resulted in solitary males wandering into East Texas. According to the Big Thicket Association, the Texas Parks and Wildlife Department has documented forty-seven reliable bear sightings in East Texas since 1977, about two-thirds of those between 1991 and 2004.

The return of black bears to the Big Thicket is testament that responsible land use in conjunction with conservation efforts can foster development while maintaining healthy ecosystems. Because of the amount of land still undeveloped in the region, there remains a real window of opportunity to create a sustainable Big Thicket and to preserve its magic.

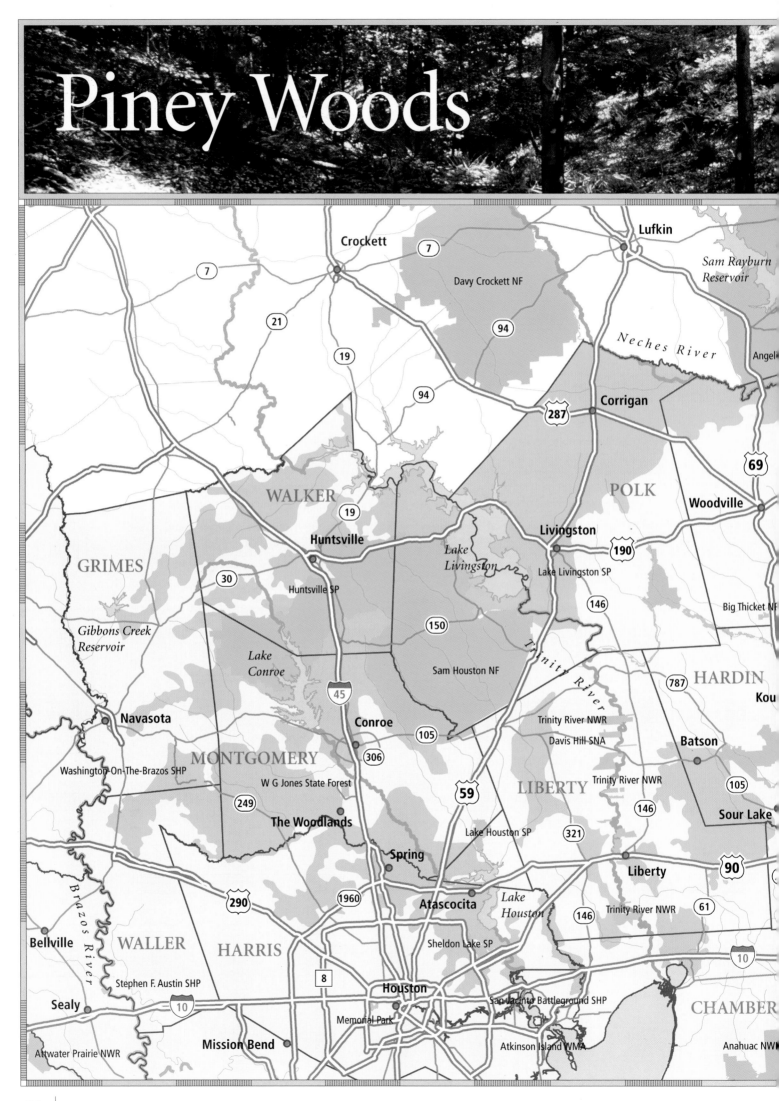

# Piney Woods

Crockett

Lufkin

*Sam Rayburn Reservoir*

7

7

Davy Crockett NF

7

21

94

*Neches River*

19

Angeli

94

Corrigan

287

69

POLK

Woodville

WALKER

19

Livingston

190

Huntsville

*Lake Livingston*

Lake Livingston SP

GRIMES

146

Big Thicket NF

30

Huntsville SP

150

*Gibbons Creek Reservoir*

Sam Houston NF

*Trinity River*

HARDIN

*Lake Conroe*

787

Kou

45

Navasota

Trinity River NWR

Davis Hill SNA

Batson

MONTGOMERY

Conroe

105

Washington-On-The-Brazos SHP

306

59

Trinity River NWR

105

LIBERTY

W G Jones State Forest

146

Sour Lake

249

The Woodlands

Lake Houston SP

321

Spring

146

Liberty

90

290

1960

Atascocita

*Lake Houston*

146

Trinity River NWR

61

*Brazos River*

WALLER

HARRIS

Sheldon Lake SP

10

Bellville

Stephen F. Austin SHP

8

San Jacinto Battleground SHP

CHAMBER

Sealy

10

Houston

Memorial Park

Mission Bend

Atkinson Island WMA

Anahuac NW

Attwater Prairie NWR

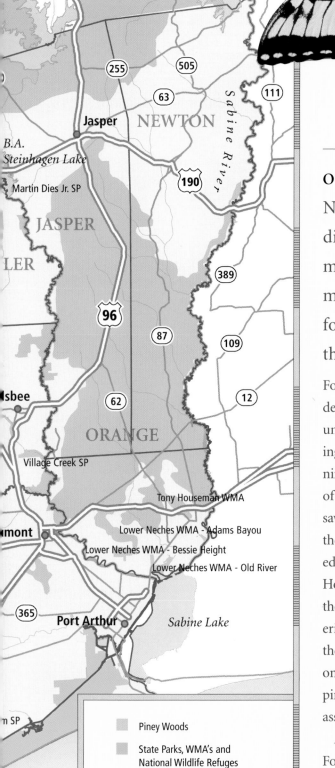

Toledo Bend
Reservoir

Sabine NF

255    505

63    111

**Jasper**    *NEWTON*

B.A.
Steinhagen Lake    190

Martin Dies Jr. SP

*JASPER*

389

96

87    109

sbee    62    12

*ORANGE*

Village Creek SP

Tony Houseman WMA

mont    Lower Neches WMA - Adams Bayou
Lower Neches WMA - Bessie Height
Lower Neches WMA - Old River

365
**Port Arthur**    Sabine Lake

n SP

Piney Woods

State Parks, WMA's and
National Wildlife Refuges

0    5    10    20    30 miles

**ON TEXAS HIGHWAY MAPS,** the Sam Houston National Forest appears as a twin-lobed green area, divided by Interstate 45 and situated about sixty-five miles north of Houston. This forest is the southwesternmost remnant of what was once a huge contiguous pine forest that ran from East Texas through the southeast all the way to the Appalachian Mountains.

For a long time the Texas pineywoods, with their densely jungled riparian areas and sandy soils, unfit for most agriculture, seemed more foreboding than welcoming. Then toward the end of the nineteenth century, as lumbering set in, huge areas of the pineywoods disappeared under the ax and saw. In 1933, with the Great Depression destroying the demand for timber, the Texas legislature invited the federal government to establish the Sam Houston National Forest. The government bought thousands of acres of cut-over forest from impoverished landowners, and while it failed to obtain all the land within the ambitious boundaries marked on planning maps, it did conserve 163,000 acres of pineywoods that are now one of the great natural assets of the Houston Wilderness.

A multiuse area, the Sam Houston National Forest is managed by the U.S. Forest Service in part

*The Lone Star Hiking Trail is a 128-mile National Recreational Trail that traverses the Sam Houston National Forest from north of Montgomery to northeast of Cleveland.*

*Left: Visitors to the Piney Woods may experience the tranquility of hiking along an old winding logging road through the sun-highlighted pines.*

for commercial timber harvest, with a portion of the profits going to Walker, Montgomery and San Jacinto counties, where the national forest is situated.

But in this forest, recreational uses dominate. It has become a playground for Houstonians. Its campgrounds draw campers and anglers. Horseback riders explore a network of trails, sharing them with riders of all-terrain vehicles and motorcycles, with surprisingly little conflict. Some trails are dedicated to biking, and off-road bicyclists make up an expanding category of visitors. Hikers enjoy the solitude of the hundred-and-twenty-eight-mile-long Lone Star Hiking Trail, which has its own hiking club that works on trail maintenance. In the fall deer hunters dressed in bright orange prowl the woods, and hikers are advised to wear the same color to prevent accidents.

The attractions of the pineywoods are plentiful. There are the trees, of course. Thousands of acres of loblolly and shortleaf pine, sometimes mixed with hardwoods, lower the temperature on summer days. On the western lobe of the Sam Houston forest, resident bald eagles nest in the tall pines and can be seen soaring over the northern end of Lake Conroe. This lake, which was created in the early 1970s by damming the West Fork of the San Jacinto River, draws anglers, many of whom stay at lakeside campgrounds such as Cagle and Stubblefield.

Bald eagles are impressive enough, but if a single creature embodies the story of the Texas pineywoods, it is the red-cockaded woodpecker. This cardinal-sized woodpecker is what ecologists call a "keystone" species: such a habitat specialist that if it disappears, we can be sure the habitat is itself disappearing. The renowned early ornithologist John James Audubon called this the most common woodpecker of the southern forests in the nineteenth century, but today it is in danger of disappearing. Only about ten thousand are estimated to remain in the southern pine forest. Perhaps a few hundred live in our region.

Named for its cockade—a tiny patch of red feathers behind the eye of the male, seldom visible in the field—the red-cockaded woodpecker draws birdwatchers to Houston from all over the world. Those who are "listers" have been known to fly into Bush Intercontinental Airport for the sole purpose of driving to the nearest nesting red-cockaded woodpecker colony in the Jones State Forest, just off I-45 only forty miles north of downtown Houston. If they arrive by about four in the afternoon and wait patiently near known roosting sites, they are almost certain to add the bird to their life lists, for this woodpecker is a creature of habit. That is both part of its charm and a reason for its decline.

Unlike other woodpeckers, which create their cavities in the soft, dead wood of a variety of trees, the red-cockaded woodpecker requires mature living pines sixty or seventy years old, in which the heartwood has been softened by a fungus called red heart. Working chiefly in the mornings after the nesting season, the birds tunnel upward through the sapwood in order to let the resin pitch drain out. Once the bird hits the dry heartwood, it tunnels down to create a rounded chamber, six to ten inches deep and three to five inches wide. Making a cavity takes from one to three years, and then may be used for several years, with the bird continually pecking holes called "pitch wells" around the entrance. The pitch wells allow the pine sap to drip two to three feet, creating a greenish blue and white cascade of sticky pitch, which is thought to deter predatory snakes. The drips give a woodpecker cavity an unmistakable appearance.

Red-cockaded woodpeckers live in family groups of from three to six birds, with one breeding male and female assisted in creating nesting cavities and raising young by one or more juvenile males called helpers. Juvenile females are driven away from the group's roosting territory, which may include several laboriously carved cavities.

When the South held millions of acres of mature pine forests that were regularly scoured by fire, the red-cockaded woodpecker could easily maintain such a specialized lifestyle. If trees in a roosting area were knocked down by a tornado, or infested with pine bark beetles, or if a cavity was taken over and enlarged by aggressive pileated or red-bellied woodpeckers, other areas were available. But with red-cockaded woodpecker habitat diminished by logging and encroached upon by development and the suppression of fire, the only chance of saving these woodpeckers is through human intervention. In trying to save this keystone species, foresters have learned not just about the bird but also about the habitat in which it specializes.

Like the pineywoods, the red-cockaded woodpecker evolved with fire. For a roosting and nesting area, the bird requires an open, parklike stand of mature pines with most of the midstory removed and the trees spaced twenty to twenty-five feet apart. In the past, this spacing was usually done by fire, which also returns nutrients to the soil in the form of ash. Early settlers of the southern pine for-

est reported many such areas through which they could easily drive wagons. These settlers, not to mention Native Americans, were known to set fires in order to clear the understory.

In 1910, when many western forests burned out of control, the U.S. Forest Service adopted fire suppression as its primary mission, embodied in its famous mascot, Smokey the Bear. But as scientific forestry grew, fire suppression has begun to be understood as a central problem in forest management, for it encourages the growth of an unnaturally thick midstory and the buildup of fuels that can eventually produce catastrophic fires. Putting this knowledge into practice is complicated as development has spread and neighborhoods have been built near and even into the pineywoods. The question for foresters now is how to use fire or to emulate its effects in order to preserve the pineywoods and the species that evolved with this kind of forest.

Forests maintain themselves through disturbance. Fire is only one means of forest disturbance. High winds, hurricanes, tornadoes, hail-

storms, droughts, disease and lightning also create disturbance. Infestations of the southern pine bark beetle can girdle and kill many trees, another type of disturbance.

Fallen trees in the warm pine forest rot quickly, nourishing a variety of fungi, which in turn provide food for spiders and insects. This insect biomass outweighs that of the other animals in the forest and provides critical food for birds. Fallen trees also prevent erosion by slowing the flow of water so that the soil can absorb it. A decaying tree can become a "nursery tree," providing a culture in which seeds sprout and grow. Standing dead trees, called snags, provide habit for woodpeckers and owls. Hollowed hardwood trees, called den trees, shelter small mammals such as raccoons.

Disturbances also create holes in the tree canopy, allowing light into the bottom of the forest, which is essential for the growth of new seedlings. A mature pine forest is not a static ecosystem; it is constantly changed by disturbances, both big and small. A natural forest is often called a "shifting mosaic," because different trees of different ages live in different places, according to light, soil and elevation. Trees start as seedlings, and grow to saplings, poles, mature trees and old growth. The other vegetation in the forest also varies, with grass, forbs (wildflowers) and shrubs creating a variety of conditions that provide habitat for wildlife.

Two pines dominate in the Sam Houston National Forest and other pine lands of the area: the loblolly and the shortleaf. The shortleaf can be

## Big Creek and Little Thicket

*In the eastern lobe of the Sam Houston National Forest, the mixed pine and hardwood forest of the Big Creek Scenic Area shows how topography and soil can shape the forest. Pines need lots of sun, and most prefer a xeric (dry) soil of the kind found in the upland areas of the forest. In such areas, the pines dominate, and the hardwoods, unable to compete for the sunlight, reach no higher than the midstory.*

*But in the lowland portions of the Big Creek Scenic Area, hikers can see how pines and hardwoods can mix. Here the soils are hydric (holding lots of water) and mesic (holding moderate amounts of water). A well-maintained trail in the Big Creek Scenic Area follows the meandering route of a creek. Here loblollies compete with magnolias and American beeches for a spot in the sunlight. The magnolias, which can survive in partial shade, are easily recognized by their broad, dark green leaves. But in competing for sun with pines, they tower seventy to eighty feet, their lower trunks bare of limbs. The smooth-barked American beeches tower as well.*

*This is woodpecker paradise, for the hardwoods provide plenty of habitat. Red-bellied woodpeckers abound, and the huge pileated woodpeckers with their pointed red crests may also be seen. A flowering vine called Carolina jessamine drapes its sweetly scented yellow blossoms atop the midstory trees. Along the banks of Big Creek a native bamboo called switch cane abounds, a sure sign of water.*

*The trail here is part of the hundred-and-twenty-eight-mile-long Lone Star Hiking Trail, which leads north to Double Lake, a camping area with two small lakes suitable for fishing from canoes and kayaks.*

*Just a few miles west of Big Creek, south of the village of Evergreen, is the six-hundred-and-fifty-five-acre Little Thicket Nature Sanctuary. This preserve backs onto the national forest and offers fifty acres of meadows and twenty miles of trails. The sanctuary is owned by the Outdoor Nature Club of Houston, a group founded in 1923. The group is devoted to maintaining the sanctuary through volunteer labor. After attending an orientation meeting, volunteers pay a small fee for a gate key and enjoy the use of a beautiful piece of the Houston Wilderness.*

*Unlike other woodpeckers, which create their cavities in the soft, dead wood of a variety of trees, the red-cockaded woodpecker,* Piloides borealis, *makes its home in mature living pines* sixty or seventy years old, in which the heartwood has been softened by a fungus called red heart.

identified by its small cones, only an inch or two long, and its namesake needles, which are little more than two inches long. The loblolly pine has needles about six inches long and correspondingly bigger cones about four inches in length. (Both of these trees can be found in Houston's Memorial Park, which is itself a remnant pine forest with an understory degraded by privet and ligustrum, invasive shrub species.)

The longleaf pine, considered the aristocrat of pines, bears even bigger cones and longer leaves than the loblolly. It is the legendary pine of the old growth southern pine forests of the nineteenth century. Longleaf pines are slow-growing, spending their first five years as little more than a bristle of needles above the ground, while sending all their energy into a long tap root that will sustain them to great heights. The longleaf was lumbered extensively and replaced with the faster-growing loblolly. Remnant patches of longleaf pine still stand in the more northern woods of East Texas, but the Sam Houston National Forest and the northern part of Houston are dominated by loblolly, sometimes called "swamp pine" because it tolerates moister soil than the shortleaf and longleaf.

To understand how the pine forest works, there is no better place to walk than the Lone Star Hiking Trail through the Little Lake Creek Wilderness Area, in the western lobe of the Sam Houston National Forest. The trail moves from the northernmost trailhead into a spacious, parklike woodland. The trilling of red-bellied woodpeckers follows the hiker all the way. Here and there one may see a pine warbler, a bright yellow resident that feeds on insects it finds by prying under the plates of pine bark. Another pine forest specialist is likely to be heard: the brown-headed nuthatch. Its call sounds much like the squeak of a child's rubber duck. This tiny bird can be seen flitting through the pine canopy, alighting on pine cones and eating the seeds.

Another scarce bird that specializes in the pine forest is the Bachman's sparrow, a plain brown bird not easily identified and a trophy for the life-listers.

As you walk down the trail, the forest tells stories. In early spring the dogwoods will be in bloom. These trees suck calcium from the ground and store it in their leaves, and when the leaves drop in the fall, this nutrient essential for loblolly pine is returned to the ground. In the understory, blackberry, dewberry, wild plum, persimmon and wax myrtle provide fruit for wildlife. Every few feet along the trail, satyr butterflies erupt and skim along the ground. These gray little fellows with the yellow eyespots take their nourishment not from nectar-producing flowers but from tree sap, fungus, fallen fruit and bird droppings. Unlike the monarchs, which feed on bitter plants and so taste bitter, making birds avoid them, satyr caterpillars feed on grasses and the switch cane that grows along the forest streams, making them tasty. Their chief defense is their coloration, which resembles a dead leaf. But look closely at the yellow-rimmed eyespots, designed to fool a predator into attacking the edge of a wing instead of the body of the butterfly. Satyrs have a beauty all their own.

Down at the south end of Little Lake Wilderness Area, the U.S. Forest Service has been burning, opening up the woods for the rare woodpecker. Trees where the birds have attempted to make cavities are marked with blue or white stripes of paint. If you stop and watch the holes in the evening, and wait patiently, chances are you will hear the birds' returning call. They will alight in the canopy above their roosting cavities, and gradually, almost casually, so as not to attract attention, each woodpecker will work its way down the trunk to its cavity. Take a good look at its back, so distinctly striped in black and white. In the fading light you will see that its markings resemble the fruit of its essential tree, the pine.

# Trinity Bottomlands

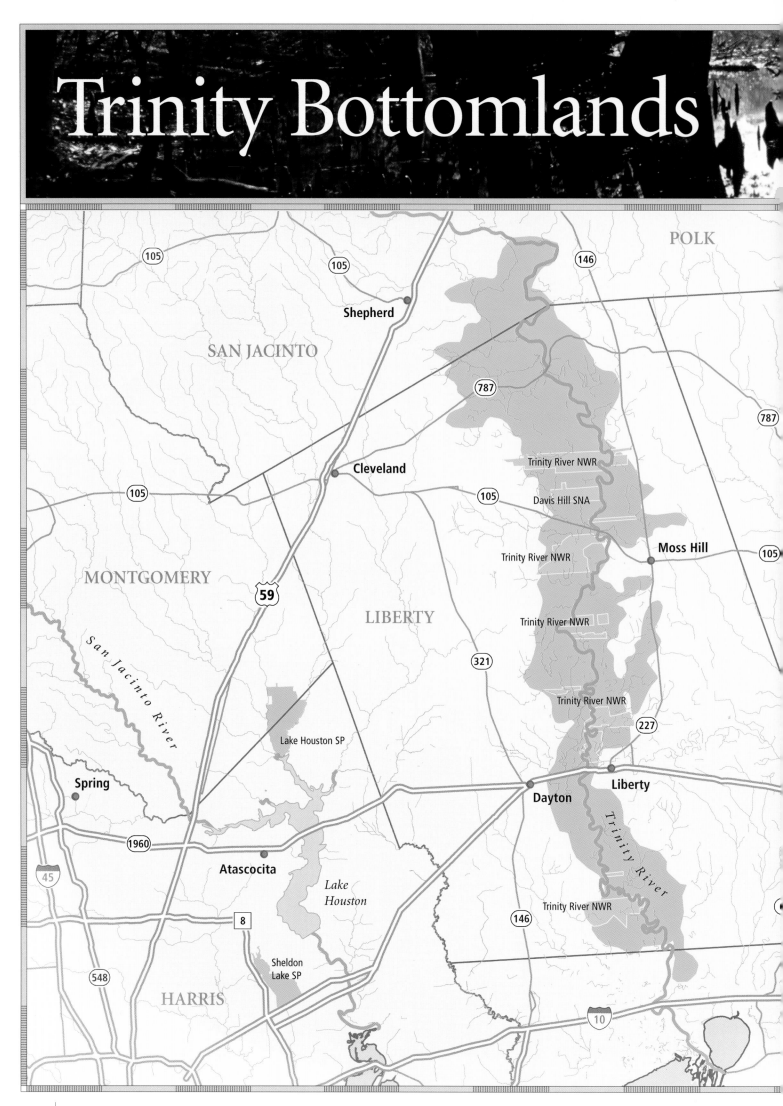

**BERNARDO DE MIRANDA Y FLORES,** a lieutenant governor of Texas in the Spanish colonial government, was a surveyor and careful observer who explored significant portions of Texas. His reports were widely used for both their geographic information and description of Indian tribes. In 1756 Governor Barrios dispatched multiple parties to the mouth of the Río Trinidad. The report by

Bernardo de Miranda was enthusiastic: "I went forty leagues along the San Jacinto and Trinidad. ... [We saw ] many plains and superior lands for planting, many woods, thick and straight, of juniper, cedar, oak, and walnut, and pines, which encircle all the plains... The land possesses luxuriant and wonderful foliage resembling straw grass... All the lands are superior and are equal in watered pastures and woods to any that I have seen and remember."

The Trinity River had been named by the earlier governor Alonso de León on a 1690 expedition; now Barrios sought information on French activities on the lower Trinity. The French explorer La Salle had met his death in 1687 near what he termed the "River of Canoes," probably the same river. French efforts to establish a presence in southeast Texas and on the Trinity had persisted until the time that Louisiana passed into Spanish hands.

*Recreational opportunities such as canoeing can be enjoyed in the Trinity Bottomlands' many miles of creeks, rivers and sloughs.*

Trinity Bottomlands

State Parks, WMA's and National Wildlife Refuges

0    2    4    8    12    16 miles

*Species found in the Trinity Bottomlands include, from top left to right: Red-winged Blackbird chicks,* Agelaius phoeniceus; *American alligator,* Alligator mississippiensis; *and the Yellow-crowned night heron,* Nyctanassa violacea. *Bottom left: Bald Cypress trees,* Taxodium distichum, *are common along waterways throughout the Trinity Bottomlands ecoregion.*

Of course the history of the Trinity begins well before European colonial activities. The Europeans found small bands of Indians inhabiting the area of the lower Trinity. The Akokisa (or Orcoquisac) lived mostly to the west of the river while the Atakapa lived mostly to the east. Ultimately the Spanish-French tensions and the presence of native inhabitants led the Spanish to establish the first significant European presence on the lower Trinity in 1756 in the form of the presidio San Augustín de Ahumada and the Mission Nuestra Señora de la Luz near the present-day community of Anahuac. Though the presidio and mission were abandoned in 1771, a later settlement that would become the town of Anahuac would provide a stage for important events in the 1800s in rebellions against Spanish colonial rule (1812–13) and in the Texas Revolution (1830s).

Indeed, the Trinity River has played a key historical role in the region, and from a modern perspective its economic and environmental roles are just as important. The Trinity supplies much of the water that makes Houston a viable city. Seventy percent of the water in Lake Livingston—a reservoir of 1,750,000 acre-feet that straddles Polk and San Jacinto counties— belongs to the City of Houston. More than twenty reservoirs have been built on the Trinity and its tributaries. It is hard to imagine Texas without the Trinity. It plays such a critical role in the state's economy. However, it is the natural qualities of the lower Trinity Bottomlands that are especially notable from an ecological perspective.

In 1840, Frances Moore Jr. offered a description of the Trinity before any reservoirs were constructed: "It is generally about eighty yards wide and eight to ten feet deep with a rapid current; at its mouth there is a broad sand bar, which is the only obstruction to its navigation. It often overflows the country, to the distance of three miles on each side. . .  Post oak, white oak, red oak, cedar, cypress, and pine, abound in the middle and northern parts."

The frequent flooding (which was more extensive prior to the construction of reservoirs) has left a tremendous mark on the country surrounding the river. The floodwaters hydrate surrounding soils and deliver critical nutrients, which support the wealth of plants, animals and landscapes described by the early explorers. Some of the remarkable features they encountered in the bottomlands are still in existence, particularly in the less disturbed areas.

Bottomlands are typically defined as low-lying alluvial lands near a river, generally featuring a forest adapted to wet soils and nutrient-rich sediments that come from flooding events. The Trinity Bottomlands run from southern San Jacinto County to northern Chambers County, with the heart of the bottomlands in Liberty County, largely south of State Highway 787, east of SH 321 and west of SH 146. The southern end runs about ten miles south of U.S. Highway 90, depending upon how one delineates where the bottomlands end and the coastal sloughs, swamps and marshes begin.

Because of the biological significance of the Trinity Bottomlands, about 105,000 acres of this area were selected in 1999 as important habitats for inclusion in the Trinity National Wildlife Refuge. Within this area, about 79,600 acres have been identified for federal acquisition from willing sellers and about 20,000 acres have been acquired.

Species counts extend to nearly six hundred and fifty plants, two hundred and seventy-five birds, fifty fish, twenty-five mammals (including beaver, otter, bobcats, gray fox, red fox, white-tailed deer and numerous bat species), and twenty-five reptiles (including alligators) and amphibians known to inhabit the areas selected for pro-

*From left to right: The American alligator, Alligator mississipiensis, and the Gray squirrel, Sciurus carolinensiss are species found in the Trinity Bottomlands year round; whereas the migratory Prothonotary warbler, Protonotaria citrea nests in the spring and summer.*

tection. Sixty-six butterfly species have been documented. Several endangered species make use of the refuge, including brown pelicans, bald eagles and the arctic peregrine falcon.

The refuge also offers shelter to numerous migratory birds, with huge numbers of neotropicals arriving during the spring migration. Well-known and colorful passerines, or songbirds, such as the vermilion flycatcher, summer tanager, indigo and painted buntings, and goldfinch can be seen along the river and in the interior forests. Numerous lesser-known varieties of warblers, vireos, wrens and sparrows including some fairly rare species, such as Henslow's sparrow and sedge wrens, also make use of the refuge. Larger colonial nesting water birds can be seen in rookeries along the Trinity, such as anhingas, roseate spoonbills and cormorants. Unverified reports of sightings of the ivory-billed woodpecker lingered on in Texas until the 1960s; the refuge's Gaylor Lake was the site of the last irrefutable Texas encounter with the woodpecker in 1904.

Five tracts of the Trinity River National Wildlife Refuge offer excellent birdwatching opportunities, with the Champion Lake Public Use Area having the most variety. Depending on the time of year, this 800-acre cypress-studded lake and the adjacent 2,300 acres of bottomland hardwood forest may yield at least a dozen species of waterfowl, plus bald eagle, swallow-tailed kite, osprey, wood stork, painted bunting, vermilion flycatcher, bluebird and numerous warbler species, including the

*Great blue herons, Ardea herodias, are the largest herons in North America and always live near sources of water.*

prothonotary warbler. Depending on water levels, one can go birding along a short levee trail or by using a small boat. Other tracts good for birding are the Butler, Brierwood, Page and McGuire tracts (directions are available from the refuge office in Liberty or on the refuge website.)

The same five tracts have good observation opportunities for other wildlife, and the Champion Lake Public Use Area again offers the most variety—nearly two dozen species of reptiles, including turtles, the venomous water moccasin or cottonmouth, various other snakes and of course alligators. Amphibians include many frogs, most of which visitors hear and rarely see. Mammals include white-tailed deer, coyotes, raccoons and an occasional bobcat. A butterfly and hummingbird

garden with a short trail is located at the top of the hill just before the pier. Wildlife can be seen from the short levee trail or a small boat.

Three tracts are prime for fishing. Champion Lake has a hundred-and-fifty-foot fishing pier, or one can fish from a boat or along a 3,000-foot levee. Fishing the McGuire tract requires a quarter-mile walk to a two-acre pond and adjacent bayou. The Brierwood tract allows access to Gaylor Lake and the Davis Bayou bank line less than fifty yards from the parking area. Bass, crappie or catfish are frequently caught at each of these areas.

The refuge has about ten miles of primitive trails scattered over five tracts. Since the refuge is primarily bottomland hardwood forest, most of it floods or has standing water at various times dur-

*An aerial view shows the Trinity River at flood stage emptying into Trinity Bay. Freshwater inflow is critical to the health of estuaries and bays.*

*A Roseate spoonbill family, Ajaia ajaja, nesting in a black willow, Salix nigra, near Alligator Bayou in Jefferson County.*

### Invasive exotic species

*Invasive exotic species pose a particular threat to the Trinity River National Wildlife Refuge. Introduced to the United States in the 1700s from China for use as an ornamental tree, the highly aggressive Chinese tallow can irretrievably damage native habitat within a few years and must be controlled. Giant salvinia, an exotic water fern originating in the Neotropics, grows rapidly with the potential to double its biomass within a week. The fern floats on top of the water in dense mats, preventing light and atmospheric oxygen from entering the water, disrupting the ecological functions of native species. Found in Champion Lake in 2000, it could choke out the entire 800-acre lake in a matter of months if not kept in check. As development approaches the refuge, care must be taken to protect it from additional exotics. Using native plant species even in developed areas both protects the refuge and offers homeowners tough, well-adapted, cost-effective plants.*

ing the year. Except for some mowing, blading and removal of fallen trees, little can be done to improve these dirt trails. Be prepared to get your shoes muddy during wet times. Some trails are loops, while others are straight in and out. Most trails are not marked, but maps are available.

Some special ecological jewels of the lower Trinity lie outside the tracts already mentioned. The Caper's Ridge area has all bottomland forest types, marshes, oxbow lakes and shallow bayous, and as its name suggests, it also has a unique geologic feature called a ridge, where the drier habitat is in stark contrast to the bottomland features. Similarly, the Wirt-Davis area has bottomland features but also offers remnant canebrakes and multiple pine ridges. The Wirt-Davis area is distinguished in having some of the highest-quality habitat anywhere in the refuge for wintering waterfowl and interior forest birds. The Demijohn Lake area, which includes Champion Lake, offers a large cypress-tupelo swamp and a naturally occurring high bluff that impounds water for long periods. Because of the very high quality of habitat in the area, it is rated the best section of the refuge from a biological standpoint.

Boating at the Champion Lake Public Use Area is restricted to boats with motors of only 10 horsepower or less or a trolling motor in order to main-

tain quiet conditions for wildlife and visitors. Canoes and kayaks, though, are always welcomed. Additional boating areas are planned as more land is added to the refuge and as funding permits.

The ecological assets and recreational opportunities at the refuge are tremendous and there is ample opportunity to expand the now primitive facilities. Trails are very rewarding but not as well marked as in some parks, and Champion Lake offers the only restroom-type facilities. Adjacent to the refuge on the west, just south of FM 2252, sits the 1,800-acre Davis Hill State Natural Area, which is remarkable for its geologic features, but remains closed to the public due to a lack of funding to develop and operate the park.

With development approaching the area, the Trinity National Wildlife Refuge should move along quickly with planned land acquisition to maintain its enormous diversity and recreational potential. For the moment the Trinity River—the longest river having its entire course in Texas—probably has more bottomland forests than any river in the state, with an estimated 300,000 acres remaining. Thanks to the conservation efforts of the U.S. Fish and Wildlife Service and its many partners, Bernardo de Miranda would surely recognize at least portions of the splendor he recorded two hundred and fifty years ago.

# Columbia Bottomland

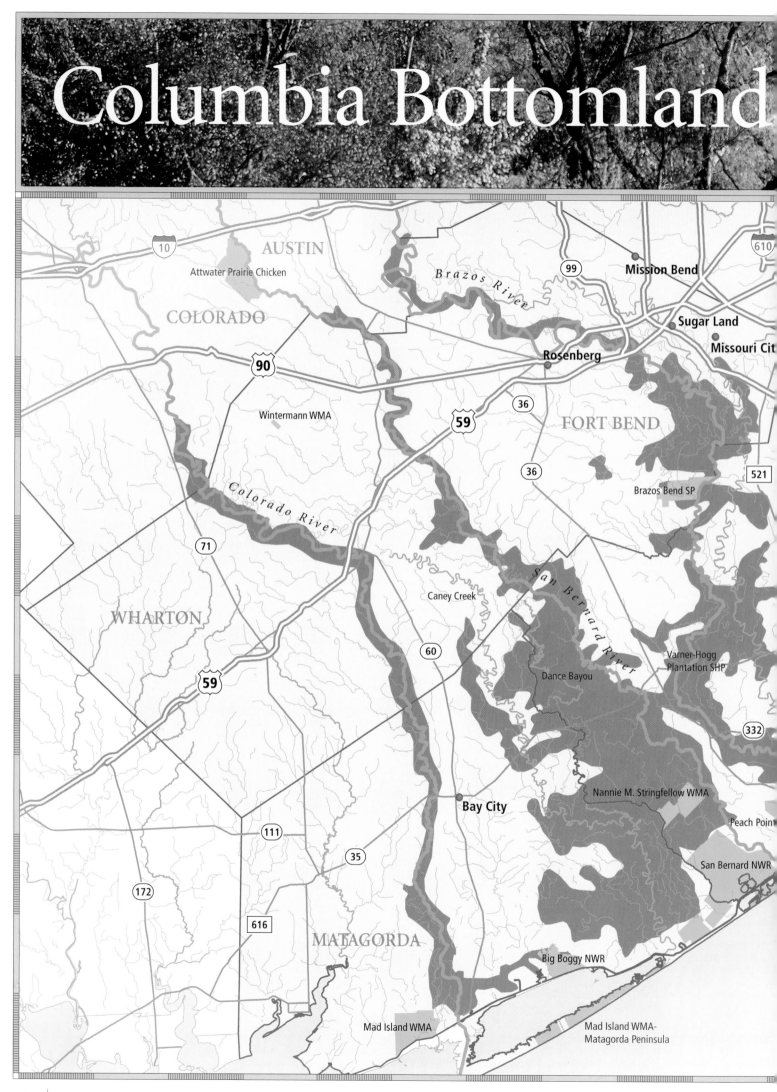

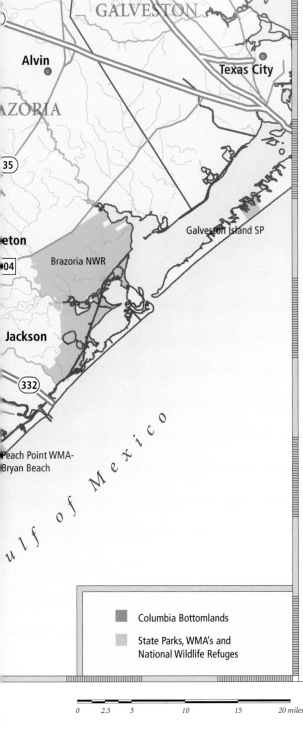

**ABOUT TWO OR THREE MILES** from the San Bernard River, in the usually wet, almost impenetrable bottomland forest, lives a tree the Texas Forest Service has declared the state's champion live oak. Its canopy, extending from a double-barreled trunk thirty-two feet in circumference, creates the sense of a huge raftered room, close to seventy feet high and a hundred feet across. This tree is old and entering its last decades. It is situated only a few miles from East and West Columbia, the first towns established by Stephen F. Austin in the 1820s. When Austin's colonies were just starting out, the tree was already well established and probably fifty to a hundred years old.

This live oak is one of the more impressive inhabitants of the Austin Woods unit of the Columbia Bottomlands—the most important stopover habitat in Texas for migrating neotropical birds. But it's not the age and the size of this tree that matters so much as what it is part of: the dense, wet, hardwood bottomland forests that have grown up in the floodplains of three rivers in the Houston Wilderness that empty into the Gulf of Mexico: the Brazos, San Bernard and Colorado.

The massive live oaks may be the big personalities of the forest, but many other trees are important: green ash, hackberry, honey locust, pignut

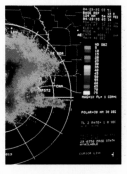

*The number of birds migrating through the Columbia Bottomlands is so large that the flocks can be seen on radar scans.*

Columbia Bottomlands

State Parks, WMA's and National Wildlife Refuges

0   2.5   5   10   15   20 miles

*Top Left: The Golden Orb Web Spider,* Nephila clavipes; *American alligator,* Alligator mississippiensis; *and the Ruby throated hummingbird,* Archilochus colubris; *all can be found in the Columbia Bottomlands. Bottom Left: Less than two hours southwest of Houston, visitors to Brazos Bend State Park can witness stunning sunrises like this one captured on film at Elm Lake.*

hickory, cherry laurel, American beech, magnolia and pecan trees, many of them draped with Spanish moss and grapevines as big as a man's arm. The flowering plants of this wet wilderness attract all manner of butterflies and hummingbirds. Sloughs meander through palmetto thickets, and the dense understory supports a lush world of orchids, ferns, frogs, snails and—most important for birds—insects.

On April and May evenings, tens of thousands of neotropical birds—the warblers, buntings, grosbeaks, thrushes, hummingbirds, orioles and tanagers, among others—take off from the Yucatan Peninsula and fling themselves across the Gulf of Mexico. With the prevailing southeasterly breezes to their backs, these birds, many of which weigh less than an ounce, fly the six hundred miles overnight, arriving at the Texas coast by mid- to late morning. If the tailwinds are brisk, they may fly a hundred miles deep into East Texas in their urgent rush to reach their breeding territories.

Should the birds encounter the headwinds of a sudden spring norther, however, they arrive at the coast and the Columbia Bottomlands exhausted and in need of fresh water, food and cover before moving on. Migration is the most dangerous time in a bird's life. Without the adequate stopover habitat provided in these key areas, many could die.

One group of ornithologists has described three types of stopover habitat: the "fire escape," the "convenience store," and the "full-service hotel." When birds encounter strong headwinds and rain, they may "fall out" and land on the nearest structure they can find. This might be a drilling platform, a ship, or a coastal woodlot. The coastal woodlots on barrier islands such as Galveston, or along the coast at spots such as High Island and Quintana, serve as fire escapes. Small as these woodlots are, they can save the lives of many birds, while giving birdwatchers intimate views of a large number of species.

In better conditions, birds use the coastal forests merely as convenience stores, loading up on protein-rich insects and snails. Such a diet is especially important to the females, which need additional energy reserves to cope with the rigors of breeding. Birds may exhaust their stores of fat completely in the effort to reach land. After recovering at a fire escape, these birds need several days of rest, food and shelter.

The Columbia Bottomlands are a full-service hotel that has been offering all three models of stopover habitat for tens of thousands of years. The only other comparable coastal forests are far to the east, in Louisiana. While much needs to be learned about bird migration, one thing is crystal clear: stopover habitat is essential, and it is declining. When Austin settled in Texas the Columbia Bottomlands covered a thousand square miles. Now they have been reduced to two hundred and fifty square miles. Neotropical bird populations have been cut in half.

Fortunately, the U.S. Fish and Wildlife Service has begun a program to save essential pieces of the Columbia Bottomlands. Working with county and state officials, the agency has managed to preserve 14,000 acres worth roughly $12 million since 1997. Money for the wildlife refuges comes from federal grants for migratory species and from private donations of land and money. The goal is to preserve 70,000 acres, with 28,000 of the total in federal refuges.

The goal is further to preserve the variety in kinds of habitats represented in the Columbia Bottomlands. Mike Lange, refuge biologist for the Fish and Wildlife Service, notes: "Each tract has a different personality based on different soil types and plants. The idea is to preserve the character of the entire ecosystem." The 46-acre palm tract, for example, contains the last remaining examples of the Brazoria palm, a native palm unique to the Columbia Bottomlands that grows up to twenty-

eight feet high. Stands were cut in the nineteenth century for use in wharves. The 5,000 acres recently added to the San Bernard Refuge includes a mix of connecting marsh and bottomlands particularly valuable because of their location at the coast.

Because it contains one of the largest tracts of old growth forest left in the South, the six-hundred-and-fifty-seven-acre Dance Bayou tract holds important clues to the character of the original bottomland forest. More than three hundred species of flowering plants have been counted at Dance Bayou, suggesting that plant diversity may be tied to bird diversity. Slight variations in soil types and ancient swales that produce small changes in elevation help create this diversity. Besides providing critical stopover habitat for spring migrants, places like Dance Bayou offer year-round habitat for other species. Biologists have collected ten years of research on wintering and breeding birds in this area.

One of the most beautiful and publicly accessible acquisitions is the 1,100-acre Hudson Woods, just north of the intersection of State Highways 35 and 521. Open to the public year-round, it offers a typical feature of the Columbia Bottomlands, an oxbow lake, a remnant of an old river bed that is probably spring-fed. Using a map provided at the parking lot entrance, visitors can take a two-mile walk around Scoby Lake and identify a series of numbered trees along the route, including live oaks, water oaks, cedar elm, box-elder maple, black willow, western soapberry, sugarberry, green ash and pecan.

Visitors will also likely see red-bellied, downy and pileated woodpeckers. The lake almost always holds ibises, snow egrets, roseate spoonbills, great blue herons, and here and there an alligator. Blue-winged teal, among the last ducks to migrate north, swim in the lake, flushing suddenly and flashing their brilliant wing patches. Back in the swampy woods to the north, wood ducks live year-round, feasting on the tiny native pecans that drop from the large trees that East Texans call "bull trees." Male wood ducks are so elaborately beautiful that their Latin name translates roughly as "bird in a wedding garment." Wary of approaching humans, they can be recognized from a distance by their wobbly flight. A Carolina wren may be heard; its loud distinctive call has been characterized as liberty, liberty, liberty, whew. A belted kingfisher may be working the lake, chittering as it flies. In winter, a red-shouldered hawk may approach across the lake to land on a tree.

### Brazos Bend State Park

*One of the most heavily used state parks in the region, the five-thousand-acre Brazos Bend State Park has some coastal prairie, but its distinction is that it sits on the floodplains of the Brazos River. Here visitors may see some of the features typical of the Columbia Bottomlands: the meandering sloughs and swales; oxbow lakes; riverbanks lined with black willow, cottonwood and sycamore; and of course, the thick hardwood forests with massive live oaks.*

*In the artificial lakes the visitor will see many alligators and probably also the nutria, a muskratlike mammal from South America that was imported for its fur and has multiplied in the wild. Along the walking paths on the levee one can see purple gallinules, bitterns, and in season, ducks. Volunteers work hard to provide amenities such as boardwalks and benches and to fight the invasive Chinese tallow. Houstonians have been known to make the thirty-mile drive from southwest Houston and climb the observation tower just to watch the sun go down while flocks of ibis wing their way past to their roosting grounds.*

The Columbia Bottomlands also hold six or seven active bald eagle nests. One such nest is situated a few miles west of Hudson Woods on SH 35 in the top of a tall oak within telescope range. The breeding pair arrives in November and broods a clutch of two to three eggs for a little more than a month. If things go well, they may raise two chicks, which must be fed and taught to hunt for three months before they are ready to leave the nest. By May, the chicks are fully fledged, and the parents move to summer hunting grounds, before returning to the same stick nest to begin the process again.

Before the eagles leave, warblers arrive. Some will move north, but for some, the Columbia Bottomlands are breeding territory. The tiny northern parula, which weighs only a quarter of an ounce, conceals its nest in the beards of Spanish moss that are so abundant in the bottomlands. The prothonotary warbler, named for a group of Catholic clerics who wore bright yellow hoods, nests in tree cavities a few feet over water, thriving on the larvae of aquatic insects and on the snails that abound in the wooded swamps.

Later in the season comes the only migrating flycatcher, the Acadian, which also uses Spanish moss or hanging leaf debris to conceal its nest. The Swainson's warbler is also a late arrival and nests low to the ground, preferring thick habitat such as laurel cherry or the once abundant canebrakes.

For every bird seen in a coastal woodlot or in bottomland forest such as Hudson Woods, many more use the Columbia Bottomlands. The magnitude of the migration drama is not easy to imagine, because the birds may stay only a day or two and then leave again at night. But there is another way to see the spring migration: with radar. Some of the most

## Canebrakes

*When Austin's settlers came to the Columbia Bottomlands, they saw not only the wooded bottomlands but also a remarkable sight that once dominated the South: a canebrake forest. The cane was one of two species of native bamboo, called giant cane (*Arundinaria gigantea*) and switch cane (*Arundinaria tecta*). Canebrakes were so thick that they provided cover for many species of wildlife. Audubon painted his famous picture of the wild turkey in its preferred habitat, a canebrake. Many folk songs allude to the canebrake. In "Sixteen Tons," a popular song of the 1950s, the singer Tennessee Ernie Ford claims he "was raised in a canebrake by an old mama lion." The canebrake was a favored haunt of black bears and a hiding place for runaway slaves as well. When Sam Houston's army retreated from the advancing Mexican forces during the last days of the Texas Revolution, they camped for a couple of days on a plantation in the Brazos bottoms. Houston's aide-de-camp, Alexander Horton, wrote of cutting runways through a dense canebrake. They felt relatively safe there, because "any approaching army would be slow moving in the terrain and would make enough noise breaking through the cane and timber so as to alert us in ample time to prepare for any encounter."*

*The canebrakes covered miles of territory and were often burned so that the land could be converted to agriculture. And the cane faced another disadvantage—cattle savored the nutritious leaves and ate the plants to the ground. Between grazing and agriculture, canebrakes all but disappeared from the Columbia Bottomlands. Two declining species are closely associated with canebrakes: a butterfly called the southern pearly-eye, and the canebrake rattlesnake, also called the timber rattlesnake.*

*Visitors to Hudson Woods and Brazos Bend State Park can see only remnant canebrake stands. Perhaps enough of this native plant will eventually rebound on protected lands for wildlife to use in a significant way once again.*

*The Columbia Bottomlands includes a diversity of tree species, highlighted in the illustration to the right, which create a rich habitat for mammals, birds and insects. The seed components of each of these tree species are also a vital food source for many species in the food chain.*

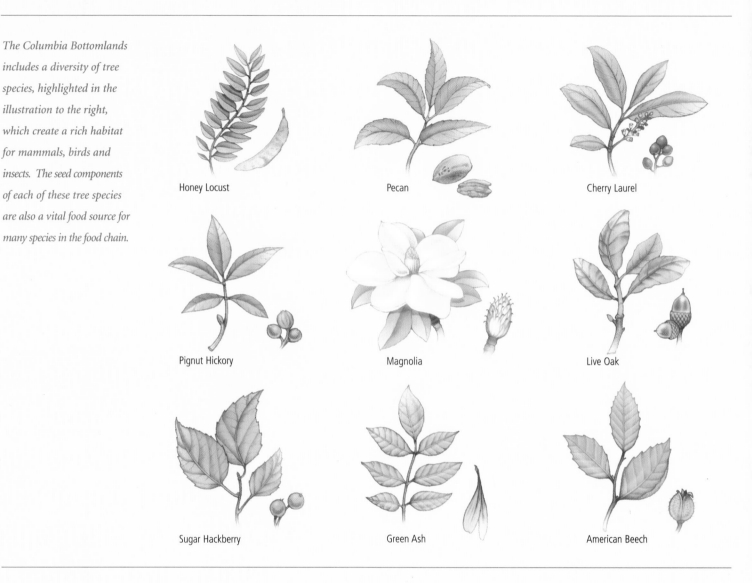

Honey Locust     Pecan     Cherry Laurel

Pignut Hickory     Magnolia     Live Oak

Sugar Hackberry     Green Ash     American Beech

influential studies of spring migration have been done by Sidney Gauthreaux, a Clemson University scientist considered the founder of radar ornithology. Using weather service radar scans, Gauthreaux has calculated an astonishing 239 million birds representing two hundred and thirty-seven species pass through the Columbia Bottomlands each spring. During the height of migration Gauthreaux estimated that 30,000 birds fly across each mile of Houston Wilderness coastline every hour.

Radar also allows one to see migration in real time. About a half-hour to forty-five minutes after sunset, when the wind is blowing from the south, the birds that have been resting and feeding in the bottomlands seem to lift off at nearly the same time in what is called an "exodus" event. A wheel-shaped swarm of as many as quarter of a million birds appears to be sweeping up from the Columbia Bottomlands and over the city.

Gauthreaux has also estimated that the neotropical songbird migration has decreased by half from 1979 to 1995. The Gulf Coast Bird Observatory in Lake Jackson is working with site partners all along the Gulf Coast, from Mexico to Florida, in an attempt to understand bird migration better. It seems clear though that preserving habitat in the Columbia Bottomlands is part of the key to restoring migration to its traditional splendor.

# Prairie Systems

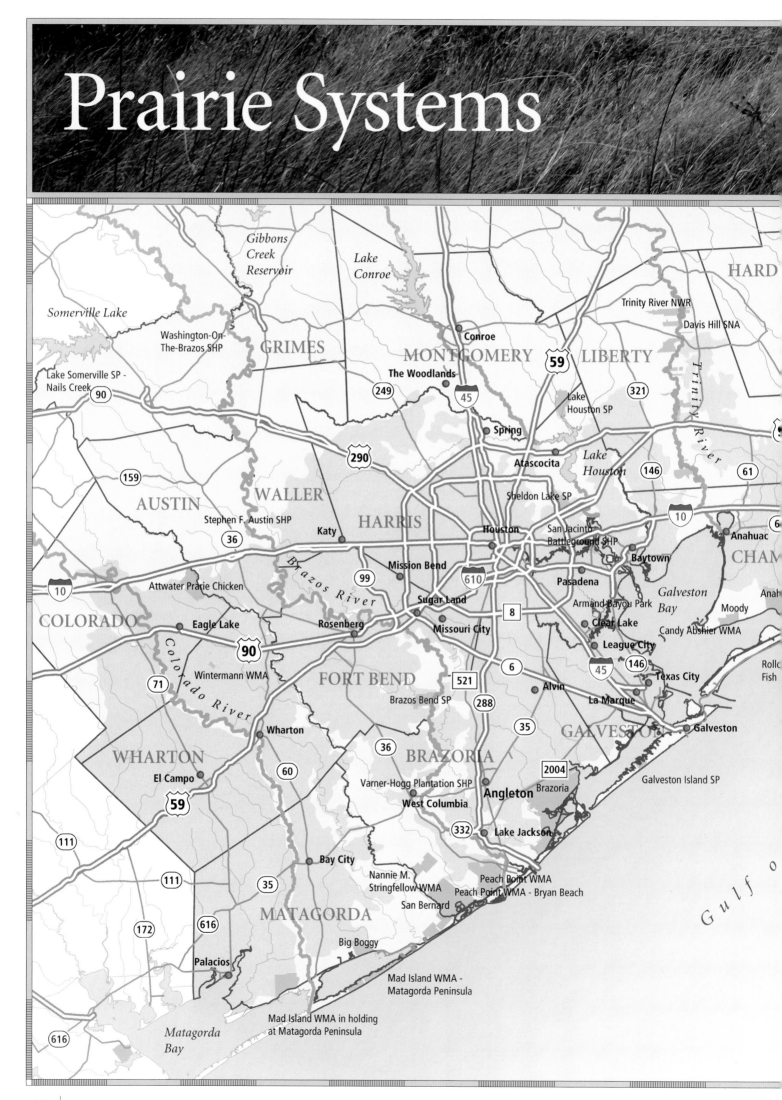

EARLY SETTLERS IN SOUTHEAST Texas described vast flat, wet coastal prairies covered with tall grasses and occasional mottes, or groves, of trees. The Texas coast once held 6.5 million acres of prairies, thick with chest-high grass that supported enormous numbers of prairie chickens. The grass was intermittently grazed by huge roaming herds of buffalo and cleansed of woody brush by fires set by nature and Native Americans.

Less than 1 percent of those 6.5 million acres of native prairies remains. Of all the ecosystems in the Houston Wilderness, prairies are the most endangered. They have been overgrazed, plowed, and otherwise developed nearly out of existence. These were mature prairies, covered with wildflowers in the spring and dominated by a mix of grasses such as little and big bluestem, switchgrass and eastern gamagrass, considered the big four of coastal prairie grasses.

Many other plants go into a mature native prairie—as many as two to three hundred. A few are easily identified: goldenrod and asters coveted by butterflies, thorny dewberry vines and the not-so-desirable poison ivy, which takes on color in the fall. Prairies are subtle. Although from a distance they may look monotonous, up close they express an intricate chain of relationships that naturalists are still working to understand, for prairies are all about biodiversity.

*The Sandhill crane,* Grus Canadensis, *is one of the few species of crane in the world that is still common and it can be seen in the Houston Wilderness area's coastal prairie and wetland areas.*

Prairie Systems

State Parks, WMA's and National Wildlife Refuges

0    5    10         20         30         40 miles

Species that can be spotted in the Coastal Prairie ecoregion include from top left to right: Nine-banded armadillo Dasypus novemcinctus, *an immature Assassin bug, of the family* Reduviidae; *and*

White-tailed deer, Odocoileus virginianus. *Bottom left: Native prairie grasses include big bluestem,* Andropogon gerardii; *little bluestem,* Schizachyrium scoparium; *switchgrass,*

Panicum virgatum; *and eastern gamagrass,* Tripsacum dactyloides.

To study a prairie is to study its plant life, but other functions should not be left out. The coastal prairies sit on level terrain made up of sedimentary deposits thousands of feet thick and covered with a slab of clayey soils known as gumbo. Such soils hold water for days, preventing floods by allowing water to percolate in slowly and enter the water table instead of running to the Gulf of Mexico. Deep-rooted prairie plants add to the land's absorptive capacity. The prairies are, in essence, gigantic flood retention ponds.

Coastal prairies, altered though they are, make up a large section of our region. They cut a swath about seventy-five miles wide along the coast, bumping into the pineywoods and the Big Thicket to the north and curving south into the Texas brush country. There are three large prairie areas: the Anahuac Prairie east of Houston, the Katy Prairie west of Houston, and the Lissie Prairie in Matagorda, Wharton and Fort Bend counties. Three major rivers—the Brazos, San Bernard and Colorado—cross the prairies, periodically flooding them.

At San Bernard National Wildlife Refuge federal land managers restored the classic tallgrass prairie of the coast. Conspicuous tall grasses such as bushy bluestem are easily identified by their feathery heads. Other grasses can be known by family rather than species. Even a grassland expert has difficulty identifying them. A grass might be paspalum, for example, but there are twenty-five kinds of paspalum, identifiable only by their flowers or by examining their seeds with a jeweler's loupe and a botany text. The San Bernard refuge, which borders the Gulf of Mexico only fifty miles from Houston, also holds salt-tolerant seacoast bluestem and cordgrasses.

Like the prairie grasses, prairie birds can be hard to identify. The ground-dwelling Henslow's sparrow, the abundant savannah sparrow, the subtly beautiful Le Conte's sparrow and the secretive sedge wren all thrive in the prairie habitat. A search along the edge of an opening in the grasses may prove fruitful when a Le Conte's sparrow flushes, then alights in a hackberry tree and poses in the morning light. This bird is evenly streaked, with an orangish throat and pale breast, a subtle beauty well worth the search. Its breeding call resembles the sound of an insect: *tzeek-tzzzzzzz-tick, tzeek-tzzzzzzz-tick.* The grasshopper sparrow, a classic tallgrass nester, resembles the Le Conte's and may flush to a shrub. Henslow's sparrow wears a necklace of streaks around its throat.

The easiest birds to recognize on the coastal prairies are the sandhill cranes, great flocks of which often visit the San Bernard refuge and may be seen feeding on the grasslands of barrier islands. Unlike the endangered whooping cranes, which require pristine coastal marshes and blue crabs for their wintering habitat, sandhill cranes eat a more varied diet, and thus are more resilient in a changing landscape. Their cries from high above are one of the great natural signals that fall has arrived.

The prairies are such a subtle landscape that we are only now recognizing their intricacy, just as they have been all but obliterated. What will bring them back? Education and conservation carried out by passionate people is a first step. One of their leading enthusiasts is John Jacob, an environmental scientist who works in Clear Lake for Texas A&M University in the Sea Grant and Texas Cooperative Extension programs.

"What makes a prairie?" Jacob asks. "It is a function of climate. Houston straddles the prairie-forest line; we get both. Drier, hotter climate gets prairies. Wetter, colder gets forests. So we see forest extending west, but only in the river bottoms. Prairies are also a function of soil; they tend to like the clayey soils, which are found nearer to the coast."

Prairie features include pimple mounds and potholes. Pimple mounds are subtle room-sized bumps about a foot and a half or two feet high that

*Flowers found in the Coastal Prairies ecoregion, top left to right: Spiderlily,* Hymenocallis liriosme*; Iris,* Iris brevicaulis*; Water lotus,* Nelumbo lutea*; Sensitive briar,* Schrankia hystricina.

were shaped by wind and water perhaps ten thousand years ago. Prairie potholes are shallow depressions no deeper than a pimple mound is high. These modest changes in elevation create biodiversity that is essential to the complex beauty of the prairie. Certain plants grow only on the drier ground of the elevated pimple mounds. One of the rare plants of the ecosystem, the prairie dawn flower, grows only on the slightly saline, sandy soils of certain pimple mounds. Prairie potholes sustain a completely different kind of vegetation. During the dry spells grasses may move in, but these areas are true wetlands. They hold seeds and roots and rhizomes of dormant wetlands plants that spring to life with the next rains, providing excellent habitat for ducks and shorebirds.

It is hard for most people to grasp such nuanced diversity in a landscape. For the last forty years, Glenn Aumann, a semi-retired professor and administrator at the University of Houston, has worked on what might be called Houston's prairie experimental center, a former World War II army camp adjacent to the Gulf Greyhound Park in La Marque, where he has 250 acres of climax prairie, perhaps the most mature and beautiful in the region. The University of Houston Coastal Center is a research center for prairies, 900 acres that Aumann believes is as valuable to the university as a library.

"How do you tell a prairie?" he asks. He drives out to his best prairie, a mile-long, one-hundred-and-seventy-acre rectangular field full of chest-high grass. By constant mowing and by poisoning

*Coastal prairies contain three times more living plant material underground than above ground. The root systems of native prairie grasses can grow as deep as 20 feet underground, helping to stablize the soil and absorb large quantities of water.*

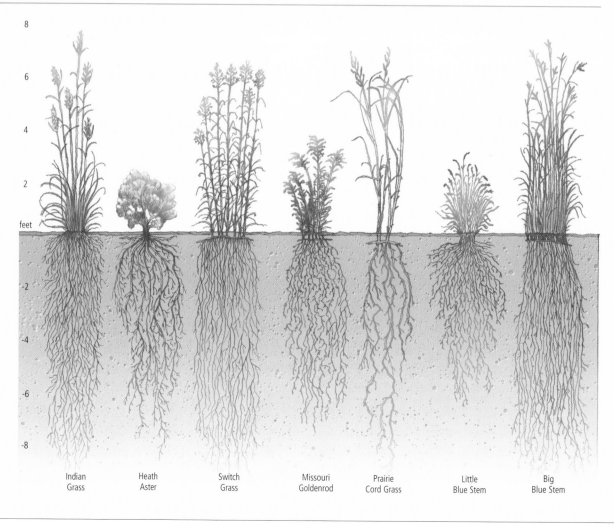

Indian Grass | Heath Aster | Switch Grass | Missouri Goldenrod | Prairie Cord Grass | Little Blue Stem | Big Blue Stem

## The Katy Prairie

Today's coastal prairies of southeast Texas are not the same natural systems that were in place when the first settlers arrived. They have been altered extensively since that time, particularly by farming and grazing. However, they still perform much of their natural ecological function. The altered prairies—the rice farms and the rangelands—are some of the best places in the Houston Wilderness region to see many of our spectacular bird species: large and graceful sandhill cranes, the carrion-eating crested caracara, large hawks such as the whitish ferruginous and the red-tailed, falcons like the merlin and the kestrel, and the magnificent wintering waterfowl.

In its natural state, the prairie with its extensive potholes was more a place of ducks than of geese. Although snow geese were always present along the Texas coast, their usage of the prairies increased dramatically with the onset of rice farming. For sheer exuberance, nothing matches the arrival of the snow geese in the fall.

Some bird migrations are quiet and stealthy, others riotous and cacophonous—celebrating their migratory success. The snow goose exemplifies the latter. The geese come south on a full moon behind the cold fronts of late October, lined up in V-formation, periodically switching leaders as they push southward. The changing leadership is highly practical as the lead bird works harder, breaking the force of the wind and cutting a path for the others to follow, a process known as "slipstreaming."

The geese know the rivers and use them for navigation, following them down to the coastal prairies and then dispersing, some going east, some west, some returning, gathering in large concentrations on ponds and flooded fields. The flocks seem to get excited as more birds arrive, the snows with their white bodies and black wing-tips, and the blues—the eagle-headed blue morphs—with dark bodies and white heads.

Aar-rik, aar-rik, aar-rik—the high-pitched calls seemingly emanate from all directions at once. Flocks are coming in—circling in a funnel cloud that extends up into the blue sky—gathering on the flooded flat, white on green, stark and clear. The incoming flights arrive in waves, wings cupped, and feet down into the wind. Some of the birds in the higher flocks get excited and "tumble" downward, literally folding their wings and dropping several hundred feet with a to-and-fro motion, opening their wings only at the last second to catch the air for a careful landing next to a neighbor: quick, efficient, graceful. The sight and sound of snow geese heralds the coming of cool weather on the Texas coast. Fall has not arrived until the first flock of snow geese is sighted, the symbol of relief after another scorching summer.

One place to view this magnificent migration of snow geese and enjoy the beauty of our coastal prairies is on lands protected by the Katy Prairie Conservancy. The Katy Prairie stretches roughly from the Houston city limits west to Brookshire, northwest to Hempstead, and southwest to the Brazos River and encompasses over a thousand square miles. Dotted with traditional agricultural operations, yet increasingly encroached upon by development, this coastal prairie is in danger. The Katy Prairie Conservancy is working toward a long-term goal of conserving 50,000 to 60,000 acres to ensure the prairie's future.

The Katy Prairie Conservancy has several preserves where there are opportunities to see an abundance of wildlife. In addition to a wide variety of birds, one can see butterflies, coyotes, hawks, quail, jackrabbits and deer, as well as hike and enjoy a respite from the city. A great spot to view waterfowl is the conservancy's wildlife viewing platform, site 100 on the Great Texas Coastal Birding Trail. Located just off of Katy-Hockley Cut-off on Sharp Road, the viewing platform affords you an excellent view of an enhanced wetland and many birds.

The efforts of individuals and organizations, like the Katy Prairie Conservancy, to save the remaining coastal prairies—the modern rice farms and rangelands—are important, even though they have been transformed from their original state of centuries ago.

the ever-encroaching tallow trees, Aumann has kept it a native prairie. He wades into the field and begins handling the grass, petting it almost as someone else would pet a dog: big and little blue stem, tridens, eastern gamagrass and switchgrass. "If you have those you are close to having the makings of a prairie," he says.

This prairie has twenty-seven different species of grass and two hundred and fifty flowering plants, he reports with pride. Last year the center sold 2,700 pounds of seed that was sent to Anahuac to reseed an old rice field. It is exceedingly difficult to restore a prairie. An old rice field can be planted with native seed and mowed and burned, and perhaps thirty or forty species will come back, says Aumann, but the whole range of plants may never come back. Yet, there is a small but important movement to reseed pastures and prairies with native grasses so that some biodiversity can return.

In spring the prairie blossoms into full glory, a shimmering field of tiny delicate flowers that will turn to abundant, windblown seed. But even in that showiest of seasons, a vital part of the prairie is never seen, for a huge amount of its biomass is underground. The roots of the bluestem, and other prairie grasses, may probe twenty feet underground, stabilizing the soil and absorbing large quantities of water. It is the native grasses that give the prairie its huge absorption capability, acting as natural detention ponds in wet times. The deep root systems are also beneficial to prairie grasses during times of drought, as they can take up moisture from deep in the soil. These native prairie grasses, with their deep and extensive root systems, are what make up the rich fertile soil that the settlers plowed up and changed forever.

One native prairie near the town of West Columbia has become something of a sacred relic. The Nash Prairie is a 300-acre hayfield of native grass that has been mowed and hayed since the first

of Austin's settlers came to the area in the 1820s. Situated along a county road north of the village of East Columbia, the Nash Prairie is part of the 17,000-acre Groce Ranch that also includes invaluable tracts of bottomland hardwood forest along the Brazos River. The ranch was left by its last owner, Kitty Nash Groce, to the West Columbia Hospital District Trustees and the tiny St. Mary's Episcopal Church of the historic town of West Columbia.

In 1999 a new pastor named Peter Conaty came to the church. He arrived with the urban eyes of a man who had grown up in the middle of Manhattan, and when he and his wife discovered the three hundred acres of native prairie, something came over them. The prairie spoke to them. One theory of stewardship says that the church should sell its land to the highest bidder and take the money to further its mission. But Conaty found something sacred in the hay meadow itself, a meadow that has thrived all these years as part of a working ranch, and plans to keep it for the church.

He asked David Rosen, a botanist with the U.S. Fish and Wildlife Service, to survey the plants. Rosen has counted close to three hundred species. To most people the Nash Prairie seems nothing very special, just a mowed, unfenced pasture where big cylindrical hay bales appear in the fall. But the native prairie and its immense diversity of species is special and there are other examples of this prairie ecosystem right within the urban Houston area.

At the top of a ten-foot high viewing platform at the Armand Bayou Nature Center, naturalist Mark Kramer looks out at what he calls one of the rarest views in Texas, a native prairie. What makes this prairie even more remarkable is that its 2,400 acres of bayou wetlands and restored prairie are smack in the middle of an urban area, right in Harris County and ringed by Pasadena, Seabrook, Taylor Lake Village and the southern fringe of Houston. These lands escaped development because of the

work of Armand Yramategui, who helped raise $6 million to save it. Visitors come to Armand Bayou mainly for its marshes and wetlands, for the chance to paddle the bayou and see big wading birds and the occasional osprey diving for a fish. But one of the essential projects of the nature center is its six hundred and fifty acres of prairie; plans are to expand this to nine hundred acres. Unlike the bayou and marshes, which tend to thrive if left alone, restored prairies need lots of intervention.

Kramer came to know the place when he was a teenager growing up in Pasadena. Now he helps manage the prairie. Fifteen thousand one-gallon pots of climax grasses have been planted here. Spider lilies bloom in one spot; they were planted too. Every year nature center volunteers collect plants and seed from places scheduled for development and bring them here. This prairie, he muses, is a living museum.

It requires constant effort to fight the invasive, woody Chinese tallow trees—imported for landscaping and now running wild through southeast Harris, Galveston and Brazoria counties. These non-natives are the enemies of prairie. Prairie grasses need full sun in order to flourish; the shade canopy of even small trees kills grass.

A primary weapon against woody plants is fire, either natural or set by human beings. Kramer hopes to burn the prairie completely every two years. Setting a fire in a prairie in the middle of an urban setting is a tricky business, but the center has been doing it safely since 1978, and now has permits to burn fifty acres instead of twenty-five acres at a time. These prescribed burns usually take place on a calm, sunny winter weekend with plenty of volunteers ringing the site, and an experienced fire boss managing the burn.

Volunteers wear knee-high rubber boots, long-sleeved cotton shirts and bandanas, and hats and sunglasses. They rub sunscreen on their faces because the ultraviolet light from the fire can burn as badly as the sun. They wield spray cans of water and long-handled "flappers" with wide rubber mats to tamp down the flames. They are constantly alert to the weather forecast for any possibility that the wind will change direction. They stay in touch with radios and identify safe low-fuel escape routes in case the fire should get out of control.

The fire boss lights the downwind edge of the plot first, creating a burned-out section of prairie called a backfire, which will keep the main fire or head fire from advancing beyond the boundaries the team wants to burn. Then the other two sides of the plot are similarly "black lined," or burned to provide a barrier. Finally the head fire is set, and the wind—(it must be a gentle one)—pushes the fire toward the backfire, where it collapses on itself and is snuffed out. The volunteers study all the embers and tamp them out before going home

Even though the prairie at Armand Bayou often holds standing water, the dry grass combusts readily and quickly exhausts itself, like paper burning. The nutrients in the thatch drop back into the ground to be reused by plants, and the warming of the soil promotes the growth of nitrogen-fixing bacteria. Everything grows up green and robust after a fire. Native Americans who lived on the coastal prairies may not have known how the chemistry of prairie fires acted, but they knew that fires worked.

Kramer often cites a passage from an early Texas explorer who compared the prairies to the elegance of vast, managed European estates—as though nature had created something so beautiful and orderly and pleasing to the eye that human hands must have made it. Such is the paradox of the prairie. What some people see merely as unimproved land is for others a carefully managed wilderness. Already the restored prairie at Armand Bayou holds about two hundred and fifty to three hundred species. The goal is to get that count much higher. An upsurge in plant species will take a while to show up; it takes time to grow a mature prairie.

## Emblem Bird of the Prairie

*At 10,500 acres, the Attwater Prairie Chicken National Wildlife Refuge sixty miles west of Houston, near the town of Eagle Lake, may seem to have plenty of land to help save a bird perilously close to extinction. "People hear that and they think it's huge," says refuge manager Terry Rossignol, "but when you're talking about prairie-chickens, it's not huge enough."*

*The Attwater's prairie-chicken, a subspecies of the much more numerous greater prairie-chicken of the Midwest, once abounded in such numbers on the Texas coastal prairies that it seemed the birds could never disappear. In nineteenth-century shooting contests the birds were stacked up in piles as tall as a man. But as the prairies dissolved into plowed fields and cultivated pastures, the prairie-chicken population plummeted to just a few hundred birds today, nearly all of them raised in captivity.*

*Rossignol's mandate is to restore a wild breeding population of the Attwater's prairie-chicken, but success is far from certain. In this effort wildlife managers are fighting invasive plants such as Chinese tallow and deep-rooted sedge and bramble-thick McCartney rose, which all crowd out native grasses. And they are fighting predators. Raccoons, skunks, hawks, owls, bobcats, coyotes, fire ants and snakes all eat prairie-chickens.*

*The problem with restoring these birds is that they evolved to fill a slot near the bottom of the food chain. Unlike the endangered whooping crane, which is a top predator and lives as long as thirty-five years, prairie-chickens are prey, and their life expectancy is usually only a couple of years. Prairie-chickens are to prairies as shrimp are to bays: food for many other species. The Attwater's prairie-chicken evolved when there were millions of acres of prairie, not thousands. By laying clutches of a dozen eggs, and re-nesting if a nest were destroyed, the birds thrived through sheer numbers.*

*They have traditionally been noted for their interesting and showy courtship displays. Each spring the males would return to the same patch of bare ground called a lek to attract the hens, which gathered nearby to watch and listen. While stomping the ground rapidly, the males inflated their yellow throat sacs, emitting a sound like that of someone blowing over the neck of a bottle. This is the "booming" that early settlers reported as haunting the prairie for days and days. When hens approached, the males tangled in brief skirmishes to establish dominance. The victor quickly bred the female, which went off to nest and raise the young by herself.*

*At the U.S. Fish and Wildlife Service refuge near Eagle Lake, no wild birds are left. They are hand-raised from incubation, moved to outdoor pens protected from predators, and gradually introduced to the wild. Teams of wildlife biologists and university interns track their daily moves through tiny radio transmitters that are placed around the birds' necks. Although every fence post on the refuge bears a row of stiff wires to discourage hawks and owls from perching, predators such as horned owls and bobcats still get their share. Considering the prairie-chickens' average mortality rate of 50 percent, Rossignol is doing well to keep a few hundred going.*

*Additional captive breeding facilities are needed to increase production and release more birds in the wild. The Houston Zoo has one in Clear Lake on land owned by NASA. Others are being raised at Fossil Rim Wildlife Center in Glen Rose, the San Antonio Zoo, the Caldwell Zoo in Tyler, Sea World in San Antonio, and the Abilene Zoo.*

*But to establish more wild birds, more land is needed. Rossignol is working with landowners near his refuge, using federal financial incentives to expand the habitat available. What is certain is that the survival of the nearly extinct Attwater's prairie-chicken is all tied up in its name. In order to survive, it has to have more prairie.*

# Post Oak Savannah

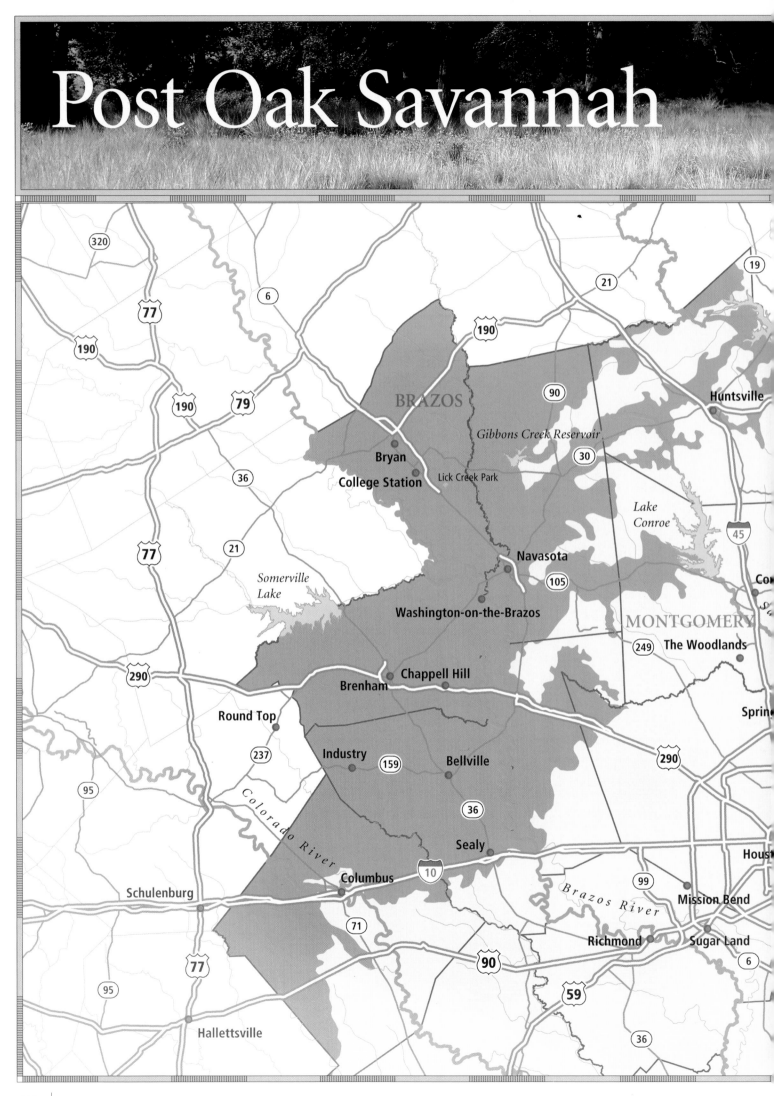

**WILDFLOWERS ARE AMONG** the great spectacles of Texas, and there is no better place to see them than in the country known as the post oak savannah. A background in botany is not required to appreciate the bluebonnets massed along the roadsides and covering hillside pastures, or the burgundy displays of the poppy-mallow commonly called the winecup, or of golden fields of coreopsis. Painters

have been trying to capture these effects since Europeans first saw them, and few parents can resist photographing their children in a roadside stand of wildflowers. Indeed, wildflower viewing is so popular that enthusiasts have created websites with maps and photographs to guide people on wildflower tours.

When Houstonians drive northwest on March and April weekends to see the flowers near the little town of Industry, or twist and turn along the two-lane road between the rural village of Chapel Hill and Washington-on-the-Brazos, they are witnessing a sight that is both natural and artificial. Many of the roadside flowers were sown by the Texas Department of Transportation, which has beautified some 800,000 acres across the state in this manner. Once established, wildflowers reseed themselves year after year, their springtime shows varying in intensity according to the

*Winecups,* Callihroe digitata, *and star daisies,* Lindheimera texana, *are a common sight in the spring along highways in the Post Oak Savannah ecoregion.*

Lake Livingston

*Trinity River*

287

177

146

770

105

321

90

59

321

8

90

61

10

65

Baytown

Pasadena

*Galveston Bay*

45

League City

■ Post Oak Savannah

■ State Parks, WMA's and National Wildlife Refuges

0   5   10   20   30   40 miles

*Left: White-tailed deer,
Odocoileus virginianus,
emerge from their resting
places to feed in the early
morning fog.*

weather. The ideal conditions are a cold winter that blocks the emergence of competing plants, followed by a wet spring that encourages the seeds to germinate and sprout. Once the blossoms have disappeared, road crews leave the flowers alone for at least a couple of weeks, giving the seeds time to develop fully and drop, ready to germinate the following year. If a roadside patch looks weedy, it is not being neglected. Its wildflowers are being conserved.

Even when their blossoms have faded, wildflowers perform important natural functions. The plants help prevent soil erosion, especially on sandy slopes. Many wildflowers are classified as forbs (fodder) and they provide browse for deer and other wildlife. Like most legumes, the beloved bluebonnet enriches the soil by fixing atmospheric nitrogen through its root nodules.

It has also evolved an interesting pollinating device. Once a visiting bee or butterfly has pollinated it, the tiny white center of the flower turns a reddish pink, indicating to other insects that no nectar is available. The pollinators appear to recognize this signal, and move on to other bluebonnets with centers that have not turned color. Thus the flowers are assured of the greatest chance of pollination, and the insects are assured of finding food with less effort. This is the timeless story of how plants and animals have evolved together.

At least five thousand species of wildflowers are estimated to grow in Texas, making precise identification a challenge even for dedicated botanists, who are constantly deliberating about the taxonomy of these beautiful plants. To complicate matters, the common names are often varied and imprecise. Many Texans, for example, call the commonly found pink evening primrose a "buttercup," presumably because of its center, which is brightly dusted with yellow pollen. Yet botanists refer to a different family, the

Ranunculaceae, as the buttercup family. The spider lily of wet meadows and roadside ditches is actually a member of the amaryllis family, not a true lily. Field guides for Texas wildflowers list sixty to seventy families. Many lovers of wildflowers content themselves with mastering the genus of flowers they enjoy, without taking the identification to the species level.

Some species present little cause for confusion. The unmistakable Indian paintbrush, for example, looks as though it has been dipped in scarlet ink. It is always seen growing among native grasses because it is semi-parasitic, drawing part of its nourishment from the grass roots. Drop the seeds of an Indian paintbrush in a flowerpot of potting soil, and they will not develop. Other wildflowers also live up to their common names. The abundant Mexican hat, also called a coneflower, bears a tall central cone resembling the crown of an old-time sombrero. The white prickly poppy often sprouts in fields and pastures, protected from grazing cattle by its spiny leaves.

These flowers and many others are the showpieces of the post oak savannah, and if their names are sometimes difficult to sort out, so is the name of the region in which they create such brilliant displays. By most dictionary definitions, a savannah is a treeless plain. How is it that this savannah is named for trees? Even the state's foremost historian of the natural environment, David Schmidly, seems uncertain about the phrase. In his Texas Natural History: A Century of Change, he calls the region both post oak savannah and post oak woodland.

These woodlands, he notes, occupy a strip no more than sixty miles wide across the central part of eastern Texas and extending in a southwesterly direction, "forming a peninsula surrounded by prairies." Indeed, the post oak savannah stretches from the Red River through the Houston Wilderness and down to the Guadalupe River. The

terrain is level to gently rolling slopes from northwest to southeast, and is used for farming and ranching. Vegetatively, says Schmidly, the post oak region is an ecotone, a transitional zone, between the eastern deciduous forest and the prairie: "The area supports a stunted, open forest dotted with small tall-grass prairies. The dominant plants of the overstory are post oak and blackjack oak and to a lesser extent winged elm and black hickory."

Frederick Law Olmsted, the landscape architect who designed Central Park, passed through the region in the 1850s. Heading west, he crossed the Trinity River. "After having been shut in during so many days by dreary winter forest," he wrote, "we were quite exhilarated at coming out upon an open country and a distant view. During the whole day's ride the soil improved and the country grew more attractive. Small prairies alternated agreeably with post-oak woods." Whether we call it a savannah or a woodland, this region has changed greatly in a hundred and fifty years, and as in the case of the pineywoods and the prairies, fire or the absence of fire have played a critical role.

The post oak is a tough, slow-growing tree that thrives in sandy, rocky, well-drained soils and can live to be four hundred years old. It features a broad-lobed leaf and horizontal branches. Its acorns provide a protein-rich food for deer, squirrels and wild turkeys. As the name implies, the post oak was used for fence posts and railroad ties before the advent of pressure-treated wood. Because these trees are drought-tolerant and thrive in poorer soils than other trees, they dominate where other trees would struggle.

Post oaks flourished before the arrival of European settlers because they are moderately fire resistant. While smaller trees are killed by fire, post oaks sprout vigorously from the root collar. With the suppression of fire, the trees once in balance with the grasslands gained an advantage.

With trees' increased canopies, the grasses under the trees failed to thrive, and the fuel loads for grass fires were reduced. Ecologists trying to restore post oak savannahs argue about how much open canopy is required in order to recreate the open woods and grasses that once prevailed.

Texas Parks and Wildlife Department managers at the Gus Engeling Wildlife Management Area are attempting to restore a post oak savannah. On this 11,0000-acre tract, situated in the upper reaches of the post oak savannah near Tennessee Colony, north of the Houston Wilderness, the state has been deliberately burning five hundred acres of post oak uplands on a regular schedule for more than thirty-five years, aiming to create a demonstration area for farmers and ranchers. The hope is that by proper use of fire, the grazing and tillage, wildlife and biodiversity can be restored. Because an estimated 96 percent of Texas lands is in private hands, conservationists believe that the best hope for conserving wildlife is to educate landowners in the techniques of combining productive ranching and farming with wildlife conservation.

Such a strategy is vital for the post oak savannah, in which there is very little public land. At the Gus Engeling WMA wildlife scientists have studied the management of deer herds closely. Deer hunting has become an important economic component of land management: hunters pay prime lease fees if deer are available. In controlled studies biologists have compared the feeding habits of deer and cattle and studied the competition between feral hogs and deer. They have built demonstration plots for farmers and ranchers, showing how to make selective clearings to improve wildlife habitat and how to raise food plots that can be used by deer, quail and other wildlife.

One of the more important projects has been to encourage farmers and ranchers to reverse a trend that began in the 1970s, when upland woods

were bulldozed to create what are often called "improved" or "tame" pastures. These are pastures planted in coastal Bermuda grass, a thick mono-culture that looks pretty from the roadside but is in effect a biological desert. Quail cannot use these grasslands, for they cannot move through the thick tangle of grass runners; as quail hunters say, the birds need to feel the dirt beneath their toes. Native grasses grow in bunches that make this possible. Under nineteenth-century farming tech-niques, quail populations flourished as forests were cut down and edges were created. Pastures held native grasses. Cover from predators was provided in fencerows. Food might be found in truck gardens (farms growing vegetables for mar-ket), besides the naturally occurring forbs.

During the last fifty years, however, quail pop-ulations have plummeted. Some quail hunters have pet theories about the cause of the decline, blaming the invasion of fire ants from South America, or even the expansion of cattle egrets. But quail biologists say the decline has been caused by loss of habitat.

It is a lesson that has proven itself again and again. Take the case of the native yaupon, recog-nizable by its bright red berries. Native Americans sought out this evergreen shrub to use its leaves as a purgative (its Latin name is Ilex vomitoria). With the suppression of fire, yaupon has invaded the understory of the post oak woods, establishing dense thickets. These thick-ets have in turn caused the disappearance of wild turkeys in the ecoregion that require an open understory in order to detect predators such as bobcats. If wild turkeys are to return to the post oak woods, the understory needs to be removed and the canopy opened up.

Still, the word is getting out about how to man-age land for wildlife. Some landowners hope to make a profit by offering deer, quail and turkey hunting. In some parts of Texas, hunting leases are already more remunerative than farming and ranching. Landowners working together in wildlife management cooperatives have shown that they can have a positive impact on wildlife. Simple tech-niques such as controlled burns and fencing cattle out of riparian areas can have an enormous impact.

College Station's five-hundred-acre nature pre-serve Lick Creek Park is traversed by several miles of walking, biking and horseback riding trails, and is one of the best examples of publicly owned places in the post oak savannah or woodland. In spring, birders come and hear the loud whistles of cardinals and the songs of wrens. Occasionally a pileated woodpecker utters its maniacal call, evoking the soundtrack for a jungle movie. Warblers and vireos work the spring canopy; indigo buntings may be passing through.

Good as it is for seeing birds, the park is even better for learning about plants. Scientists from Texas A&M University have inventoried the park's vegetation and have created a website offering a virtual tour with pictures and expla-nations (http://www.csdl.tamu.edu/FLORA/ftp/fieldtrips.htm). Lick Creek Park offers a mix of habitats, including bottomland creeks, a wet sedge meadow, and small blackland prairies invaded by yaupon.

The post oaks are easily identified by their broad, twin-lobed leaves, sometimes resembling a cross. In winter the post oaks are recognizable by their crooked branches and irregular canopy. Resurrection ferns cling to the branches of the post oaks, brown and desiccated during dry spells, vibrant and green after rains revive them. These ferns are epiphytic rather than parasitic and do not harm the tree. Many fruit-bearing plants thrive in the understory, including dew-berries, which grow from fibrous vines close to the ground, American beautyberry, farkleberry, and

*Common wildflowers of the post oak savannah in the Houston Wilderness region.*

Wine-cup

Spider Lily

Camphor Daisy

Bluebonnet

Passion Flower

Primrose

Coreopsis

Texas Paintbrush

Texas Lantana

wild mustang and muscadine grapes all abound.

And the wildflowers are impressive. All the usual suspects are here: bluebonnets, Indian paintbrush, Indian blanket, winecups and evening primroses. Don't overlook smaller common jewels such as herbertia, a small blue iris bearing three "tepals," a combination of petals and sepals. In damp places are masses of yellow buttercups.

One of the treasures of the park is a wild orchid called the Navasota ladies' tresses. This endangered orchid appears in only a few Texas counties and is a specialist of the post oak woods. Like many orchids, it produces leaves in the spring, which gradually wither and die, providing nourishment that enables the plant to produce a single stalk of small white or creamy to green flowers in the fall. Not much is known about this self-pollinating orchid, which appears in scattered spots and is easily confused with a more common orchid.

But this is precisely the fascination of plants. Although they can seem overwhelming in their variety and complexity, they soon reward those who try to understand them, yielding insights about how the intricate interactions of the natural world work. And, of course, in their exuberant shows of color, they reward everyone else too.

# Estuaries & Bays

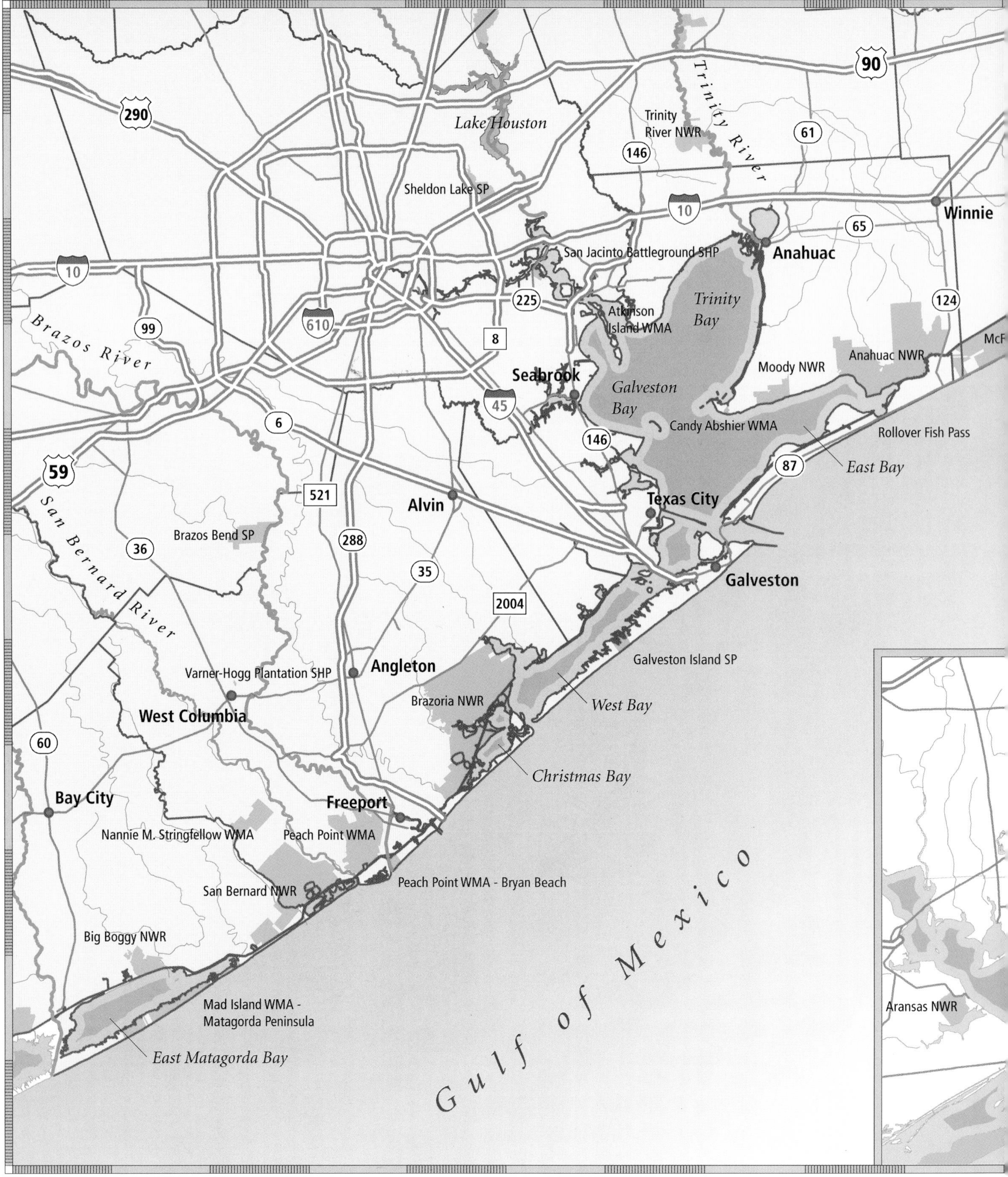

290

Lake Houston

Trinity River NWR

Trinity River

90

146

61

Sheldon Lake SP

10

Winnie

65

San Jacinto Battleground SHP

225

Anahuac

124

Atkinson Island WMA

Trinity Bay

McF

10

Brazos River

99

8

Moody NWR

Anahuac NWR

610

Seabrook

Galveston Bay

Candy Abshier WMA

Rollover Fish Pass

6

45

87

East Bay

146

59

521

Alvin

Texas City

San Bernard River

Brazos Bend SP

288

36

35

Galveston

2004

West Columbia

Varner-Hogg Plantation SHP

Angleton

Galveston Island SP

Brazoria NWR

West Bay

60

Christmas Bay

Bay City

Freeport

Nannie M. Stringfellow WMA

Peach Point WMA

San Bernard NWR

Peach Point WMA - Bryan Beach

Big Boggy NWR

Gulf of Mexico

Mad Island WMA -
Matagorda Peninsula

Aransas NWR

East Matagorda Bay

Lower Neches WMA

rt Arthur

*Sabine Lake*

D. Murphee WMA

Sabine Pass Battleground SHP

Sea Rim SP

Texas Point NWR

Bay City

Nannie M. Stringfellow WMA

Big Boggy NWR

acios

*East Matagorda Bay*

Matagorda Bay Nature Park

Mad Island WMA in holding at Matagorda Peninsula

tagorda

Houston Bays

State Parks, WMA's and National Wildlife Refuges

atagorda and NWR

**A GULF OF MEXICO ESTUARY** has a definite geometry, a pairing of one river or several with a pass or passes connecting the bay to the Gulf. Within the last few thousand years—just the other day, geologically speaking—the sea level was about two hundred feet lower than it is today. In places the coastline was dozens or hundreds of miles farther out into the Gulf than it is now. As frozen water was unlocked when the last ice age retreated, the Gulf began to rise to its current level, flooding river valleys that had cut into the shelf.

Three of these flooded river valleys became the three great estuaries of the upper Texas coast: the Sabine Lake system that we share with Louisiana; the Galveston Bay system south and east of Houston; and the Matagorda Bay system to the southwest. Over time, river and Gulf sediments formed barrier islands paralleling the coast and almost blocking the mouths of flooded valleys, so that only one or two openings allow the energy from the uplands to flow through the bays and into the Gulf. We have been slow to appreciate what tremendous natural resources these water bodies are.

Sabine Lake receives its fresh water from the Sabine and Neches rivers and Taylor Bayou and is connected to the Gulf by Sabine Pass. Galveston

*The Black-crowned night heron,* Nycticorax nycticorax, *a resident of our estuaries, stalks its prey at night, hence its name.*

0   2.5   5   10   15   20   *25 miles*

*Left: A lone fisherman cast-nets for bait near Matagorda. Recreational fishing is a favorite pastime and important industry in the Estuaries & Bays ecoregion of Houston Wilderness.*

Bay is fed by the Trinity and San Jacinto rivers and numerous smaller creeks and bayous and is linked with the Gulf via the Bolivar Roads, San Luis Pass, and through the artificial cut called Rollover Pass. Matagorda Bay receives inflow from the Colorado and Lavaca rivers and several other creeks and bayous and is connected with the Gulf via the artificial channel at the Port O'Connor jetties and Mitchell's Cut to East Matagorda Bay near Sargent.

San Luis Pass is a dynamic place with 20 percent of the tidal flow for all of Galveston Bay moving through it. The sand bars around the pass change with each storm, causing changes in the pattern of water movement. When the tide is going out the water moves very quickly, and when the current hits the southerly longshore current that flows in the summertime, dangerous rip currents are produced. More people have drowned near San Luis Pass than at any other site along Texas' beaches.

Coastal hydrologist Dr. George Ward, of the University of Texas Water Resources Center in Austin, has described estuaries as a salad bar because of the immense natural productivity typical of their high-energy areas. An estuary converts tremendous amounts of sunlight into food through the photosynthetic action of microscopic plants called phytoplankton, which make up a veritable salad bar for bay organisms to graze upon.

An estuary such as Galveston Bay converts as much carbon dioxide into plant material as does a tropical rain forest. However, there is one huge difference. In the rain forest the carbon dioxide becomes the leaves and wood of trees, but in an estuary the carbon dioxide is converted into microscopic plants, which are immediately eaten by other organisms, supporting life within the estuary by passing the sun's energy up the bay food chain to other forms of life.

These microscopic plants flourish in the estuary because the freshwater inflow brings with it nutrients such as nitrogen and phosphorus and silica that allow the tiny plants to grow. The bays of the Houston Wilderness area receive the highest inflows of any estuaries on the Texas Coast. Sabine Lake in water-rich East Texas receives over 12 million acre-feet of water inflow per year, and the Galveston Bay system receives just over 10 million acre-feet of inflow. By contrast, Matagorda Bay receives only about 2 million acre-feet, reflecting the sharp decline in rainfall as one moves south and west in Texas.

An acre-foot is a lot of water: 325,000 gallons. In gallons, Sabine Lake and Galveston Bay receive 3.9 and 3.2 trillion gallons of freshwater inflow respectively, with Matagorda Bay receiving 650 billion gallons. The fresh water flowing in is a defining element of our estuaries, the places where fresh and salt water meet, and it is essential to their productivity.

A significant amount of scientific research has been conducted regarding the amount of fresh water that is absolutely necessary to maintain the bays' productivity. To date, estimates have been based upon computer models developed by the Texas Parks and Wildlife Department and the Texas Water Development Board. However, it is not easy to understand or describe mathematically the interrelated workings of the estuarine food chain.

Simply stated, the food chain of an estuary is one of the marvels of nature. Microscopic phytoplanktons are tiny plants eaten by microscopic animals called zooplankton as well as by higher organisms such as oysters. Both the phytoplankton and zooplankton are fed upon by larval shellfish, such as the early life stages of crabs and shrimp, as well as by juvenile finfish such as croaker, mullet and many more. In turn, larger fish feed upon the juveniles. At the top of the food chain are the predators, such as the trout and redfish that support our popular sport fishery and the crabs that end up in local restaurants.

One difficulty in modeling this system is the large number of variables that must be considered. There is variability in rainfall and thus in inflow quantity and quality. There is the need to collect biological data describing all elements of the system, from the microscopic plants to the large predators. And one has to explain away any other factors that might limit productivity in one bay in one year—a hurricane, perhaps, or a period of prolonged cold.

But make no mistake—our bays and estuaries are incredibly productive. Galveston Bay is the national leader in the production of oysters. Port Arthur, Galveston and Palacios lead the Texas coast in shrimp landings, and Texas leads the nation in brown shrimp landings. Together, Sabine Lake and Galveston and Matagorda bays provide over half of the blue crab catch on the Texas coast. And for recreational fishing, Galveston Bay—the most heavily fished of our coastal bays—also has the highest catch per unit of effort by sport fishermen.

One of the best ways to begin to grasp the productivity of an estuary is to take a trip designed with this as its objective. Among the best of these are the excursions conducted by the nonprofit Waterborne Education Center operating out of Anahuac, which performs the important function of educating schoolchildren as well as the general public about the roles and functions of the bays. Private guides based around Matagorda Bay and Sabine Lake lead both scheduled and customized ecology tours by boat and kayak—an Internet search will turn up current offerings out of Galveston, Palacios, Bay City and Orange.

A Waterborne Education Center trip takes in both the shallow and deepwater habitats of Trinity Bay. Chambers and Jefferson County Marine Agent Terri Ling is among those who guide such excursions, offering her considerable knowledge. In the shallow waters off Smith Point, the peninsula dividing Trinity Bay from East Bay, Terri asks for a volunteer to help her pull a seine near the edge of the marsh.

The seine is a small-mesh net with weights to hold one side of it on the bottom and floats to suspend the net within the water column. On either end are poles. One person stays near the shoreline while the other takes the net out away from the shore and then brings it back in a wide arc, encircling whatever is between the net and the shore. The suspense builds as the net nears the shore. With a flourish, the weighted bottom is slid up the bank, trapping the small organisms of the estuary edge. Immediately, hundreds of small brown shrimp are hopping in the net, along with several small finfish of different species, likely including flounder. The catch in the net is carefully emptied back into the water after everyone has understood how much life seethes in the shallows near the edge, and the visitors move back to the large boat that is the bay home of the Waterborne Education Center.

The Chambers-Liberty Navigation District bought two old U.S. Coast Guard buoy tenders and leased them to the center for educational usage. Each boat can accommodate about forty passengers and is rigged to pull nets that capture the organisms of the deeper waters of the bay system.

The first try may be with a plankton net, which has very fine mesh intended to trap the microscopic organisms that fuel the food chain. After a minute or two, the net is pulled in and its contents are emptied into a jar: a soupy-looking mixture. This soup is what we can see of the microscopic plants and animals, visible only by their interference with light penetrating the water.

The next try may be with the larger trawl net, similar to the kind used on shrimp boats. Guides test the salinity of the water, which may be quite low if there have recently been rains intensifying

the freshwater inflow. In that case the trawl for this day may reveal a relatively meager harvest of shrimp and finfish, reflecting the response of the estuarine organisms to sudden incoming fresh water. The catch results further illustrate some of the difficulties of modeling the activity in the bays since estuarine organisms move, responding to pulses of fresh water or to increases in salinity.

The organism that most clearly reflects the chameleon character of the estuary is the oyster, a wonderful example of adaptation to the estuarine environment. Mature oysters are immobile, encased in calcite shells that cement to clay and to each other to form reefs in the Sabine, Galveston and Matagorda systems. They feed by pulling water in and filtering out microorganisms that are floating in the water column, rather like the operation of our plankton net.

Oyster reefs are found in that portion of a bay that is neither too fresh nor too salty. In the Sabine Lake system, they are found in the southern end of the lake nearer to Sabine Pass, reflecting the high volume of inflow and the relatively small size of Sabine Lake. In Galveston Bay, the oysters are found nearer the middle of the bay system, with large reefs also appearing in East and West Bays. In the Matagorda Bay system, the reefs are in the process of reestablishing themselves in response to the man-made diversion of the Colorado River and the new salinity regimes that have followed that attempt to increase productivity by ensuring that more fresh water reaches Matagorda Bay.

Although the mature oyster is immobile, its reproductive strategy provides for options and adaptation. Millions and millions of eggs are released and fertilized, and they can disperse and settle throughout the estuary. In average years the main reefs are where the young oysters, called spat, will settle and grow. During a dry year when the bay is saltier, the spat settle and thrive closer to the

freshwater inflow. And in a wet year with a fresher bay, the spat settle and thrive closer to the outlet to the Gulf. In this way the oyster is able to adjust to conditions, but note that young oysters need freshwater inflow in order to thrive.

The oyster reef is a center of biological diversity in our bays. It provides habitat for smaller finfish. It provides attack points for predators. Where oyster reefs extend close to or above the water line, they provide excellent fishing stations for fish-eating birds. In any of our bays, biological action abounds on and around the oyster reefs.

Humans have intervened in many ways to alter our estuaries. These water bodies are relatively shallow, with a natural depth of approximately ten feet in the deeper portions. Navigation through the passes and reefs was quite dangerous and was limited to shallow-draft vessels prior to the construction of navigation channels through each of the bay systems. Today Sabine Pass has been deepened to forty feet to provide navigation to Port Arthur, Beaumont and Orange; Bolivar Roads has been deepened to forty-five feet to provide navigation to Galveston, Texas City and Houston; and an artificial channel has been constructed at Port O'Connor to provide deepwater navigation to Point Comfort and Port Lavaca on Matagorda Bay.

As a result of this channelization, natural passes are rarer than they once were. In the Houston Wilderness area only two natural passes still exist—San Luis Pass at the southern end of Galveston Island and Pass Cavallo on Matagorda Bay near Port O'Connor. And of these two, Pass Cavallo is slowly silting in because most of the interchange between Matagorda Bay and the Gulf flows through the artificial cut at the Port O'Connor jetties.

Among the upper coast bay systems, none has been modified by humans to the extent that Matagorda Bay has been. In the 1930s, the

Colorado River emptied into it at Matagorda. However, a major logjam upstream was causing flooding on the river. When the U.S. Army Corps of Engineers blew up the logjam, the silt and other debris rapidly formed a delta into the bay, causing a different flooding problem at Matagorda. To remedy this problem, a channel was constructed through the isthmus that connected the mainland to Matagorda Peninsula on the Gulf side of the bay. For several decades the Colorado River thus flowed directly into the Gulf.

In the late 1980s the U.S. Fish and Wildlife Service, Texas Parks and Wildlife and the Corps of Engineers determined that productivity in the bay could be improved if the river were diverted into Matagorda Bay. A diversion channel was constructed in 1991, and a major flood occurred shortly thereafter, forever changing the geometry of Matagorda Bay. Today, a new delta is being built into the bay. The diversion channel is disgorging tons of sediment along with hundreds of large trees that lined the channel. This is an active geological process set in motion by human intervention.

At the south end of Matagorda Bay, a different type of intervention has occurred. At the Port O'Connor jetties, the channel that was dug out to a depth of forty feet has been deepened by the currents to more than one hundred feet. In turn, this deeper channel is interfering with the movement of larval shrimp and crabs and finfish, because they move with the tides and drop to the bottom of the passes to hold on during tidal changes. With such a deep channel, the bottom cannot easily be found, and the organisms get washed back to the Gulf.

The migration of larval fish and shellfish from the Gulf to our bays and estuarine nurseries is one of many phenomena that have been documented but that remain poorly understood. The success of these species depends upon the movement of their larval forms from the Gulf to the bay and into the sheltering nursery areas where they are nourished and grow into mature organisms. If they do not reach these nurseries, the species will not survive.

As the birdwatchers of the world have long since been aware, the rich fish and shellfish resources of our bays make them attractive to many types of fish-eating birds. During the winter months, sea ducks such as mergansers and buffleheads can be found around the bay systems, along with wintering white pelicans and native brown pelicans. With the advance of spring the islands are astir with the noisy nesting activity of colonial water birds—herons, night-herons, egrets, pelicans, cormorants, gulls, terns and skimmers.

In the spring, there is nothing quite like paddling a kayak on Christmas Bay or Drum Bay, near the nesting sites of these magnificent water birds at the southwestern end of the Galveston Bay system. The birds are dazzling during breeding season. Roseate spoonbills, an unlikely and outrageous bright pink, compete for nesting space among the salt cedars with the dark cormorants and the flashing white great egrets.

At the grassy end of an island, the heads pop up as a kayak quietly moves past. One after another, tricolored herons reveal a purple neck and a single extended white head feather. Black-crowned night-herons crouch and watch with a wary red eye from the low brush next to laughing gulls paired on the shell beach. At the end of the rookery island, standing on exposed sand and shell, may be a pair of oystercatchers, their orange-red bills in startling contrast to black heads.

Paddling, fishing or birding in an estuary, one begins to grasp the richness of the surrounding life, birds swirling, brown shrimp jumping in the shallows, schools of mullet moving the water before the kayak. Our bays and estuaries are living, vibrant systems that have immense value to us ecologically, economically and recreationally.

# Coastal Marshes

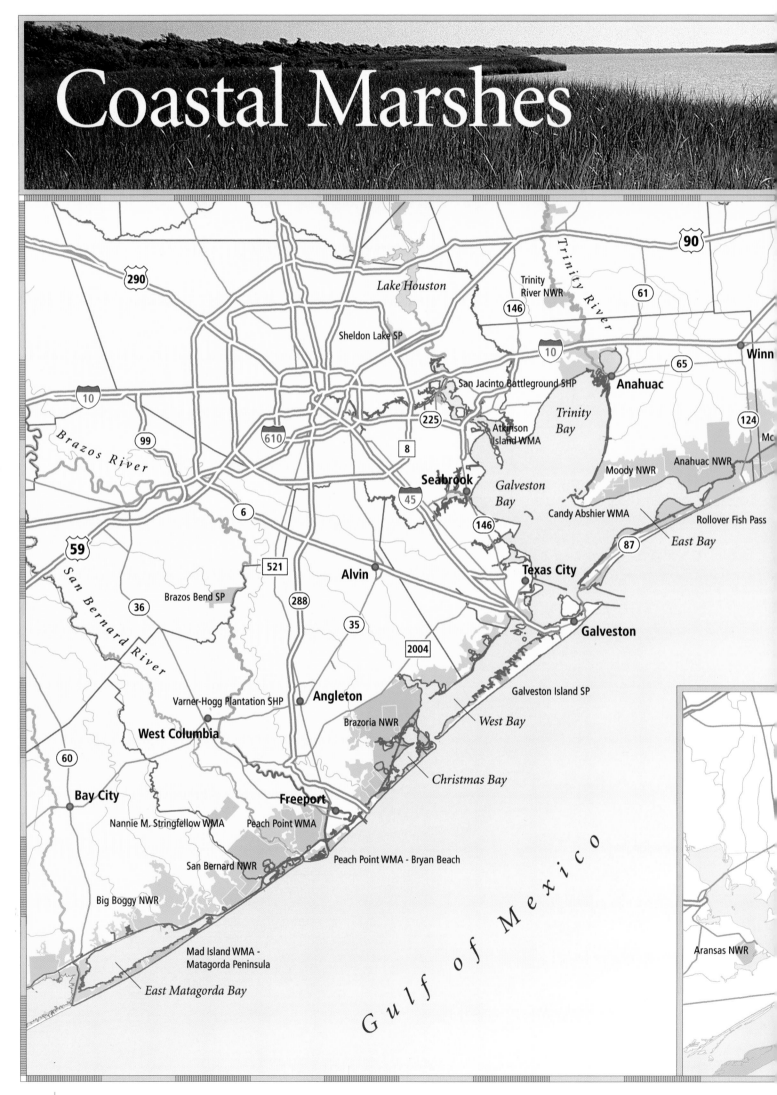

290

Lake Houston

Trinity River NWR

90

61

146

Trinity River

10

Sheldon Lake SP

San Jacinto Battleground SHP

Anahuac

65

Winn

10

225

Atkinson Island WMA

Trinity Bay

124

Mc

99

8

Brazos River

Moody NWR

Anahuac NWR

Seabrook

Galveston Bay

45

6

146

Candy Abshier WMA

Rollover Fish Pass

East Bay

87

59

521

Alvin

Texas City

36

Brazos Bend SP

288

35

Galveston

San Bernard River

2004

Galveston Island SP

Angleton

West Bay

Varner-Hogg Plantation SHP

Brazoria NWR

West Columbia

Christmas Bay

60

Bay City

Freeport

Nannie M. Stringfellow WMA

Peach Point WMA

San Bernard NWR

Peach Point WMA - Bryan Beach

Big Boggy NWR

Gulf of Mexico

Mad Island WMA - Matagorda Peninsula

Aransas NWR

East Matagorda Bay

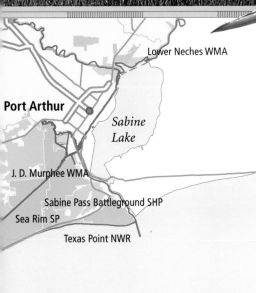

Lower Neches WMA

**Port Arthur**

*Sabine Lake*

J. D. Murphee WMA

Sabine Pass Battleground SHP

Sea Rim SP

Texas Point NWR

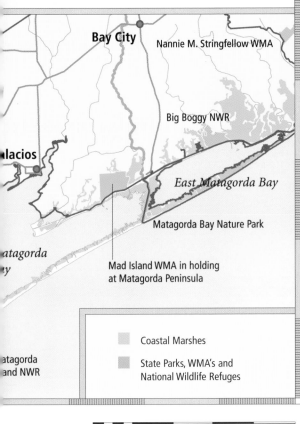

**Bay City**    Nannie M. Stringfellow WMA

Big Boggy NWR

lacios

*East Matagorda Bay*

Matagorda Bay Nature Park

atagorda
y

Mad Island WMA in holding
at Matagorda Peninsula

Coastal Marshes

State Parks, WMA's and
National Wildlife Refuges

atagorda
and NWR

**THE BAYS AND ESTUARIES** of the upper Texas coast are rimmed by marshes from the Louisiana border to the western shoreline of Matagorda Bay. These grasslands are true wetlands—part water, part land—that provide a transition zone between the upland prairies and the open water of the bays.

All wetlands are not created equal. There are three major types of marshes on the Texas coast. Salt marsh touches the salty water of the bays; true freshwater marshes are found adjacent to the prairies, mostly in the Sabine Lake area. The third type is the brackish or intermediate marsh, a transitional grassland characterized by plants that can tolerate both salty and fresh conditions. Each of these systems provides different natural functions.

A good way to appreciate the marshes fringing the coast is from the air. Looking down on them, one sees an interconnected web of grasslands with areas of shallow open water. This strip is narrowest in the southern portion of the Houston Wilderness, adjacent to Matagorda Bay, and gradually widens as one moves through the Galveston Bay system to the Sabine Lake system near Port Arthur and Beaumont. East of Sabine Lake, the strip widens into the Sabine National Wildlife Refuge of southern Louisiana. The refuge contains

*Coastal marshes are rich habitat for many species of fish, making the marshes a favorite for recreational fishermen.*

0    2.5    5    10    15    20    25 miles

*Species of the Coastal Marshes ecoregion from top left to right: Black-crowned night heron,* Nycticorax nycticorax; *Water lilies,* Nymphaea odorata; *Purple Gallinule,* Porphyrula martinica.

*Bottom left: A typical coastal marsh scene: a breeze ruffles the marsh grass and creates ripples on the calm water.*

salt, brackish and freshwater marshes and connects with an even wider band of marshes reaching eastward across south Louisiana.

In contrast to the coastal marshes, the wetlands that dot the inland prairie are commonly referred to as pothole wetlands. Prairie potholes are freshwater wetlands and have the same vegetation types as the freshwater marsh. Pothole wetlands, however, are dots within a larger prairie fabric and may be wet only intermittently (see the chapter on prairies), while the marshes described here are great swaths of saturated coastal landscape.

Swamps and floodplain bottomlands are also wetlands, but they are forested wetlands rather than grasslands. Swamps have water during most of the year, whereas floodplain bottomlands are inundated only by larger flood events, although they often include depressional swamps and oxbow lakes. The large swamps of the Houston Wilderness are on the Trinity River, and the major floodplain bottomlands of the region are the Columbia Bottomlands (see those chapters for fuller discussion).

Marshes are difficult places for people. Walking is hard. The marsh grass is rooted in dark, mushy soils called hydric soils, which sometimes emit sulfurous gases when you step onto and penetrate the muck that grabs your foot and causes you to leave your shoe behind. Marshes are places for birds that can walk on the leaves lying on the water's surface and for long-legged wading birds, waterfowl, fish and alligators. The best way to get into a salt marsh for closer observation is in a kayak. Marsh kayaking is a novel and expanding form of outdoor recreation on the coast, full of subtle pleasures. Though the salt marsh is adjacent to the open water of bays, the water is shallow. Sometimes you kayak in water less than a foot deep.

Smooth cordgrass, Spartina alterniflora, is the primary species of our salt marshes. Spartina is emerald green in the spring and golden green in the

fall, a beautiful contrast to the blue bay water. Cordgrass can cover hundreds of acres at a single location, disappear when a higher piece of ground intrudes, and then reappear for several hundred acres more, a pattern recurring throughout the upper coast bays.

The Spartina marsh is laced with tidal channels and is punctuated with open lakes. Along the Texas coast the tides are relatively small in range, varying only one to two feet between the low and the high, with the highest tides coming in spring and fall and with tropical storms. At high tide the water comes up the channels and spills over onto the adjacent marsh, flooding the grass with several inches of water that covers the roots and inches up the stems. During higher high tides the entire marsh is flooded with a foot of water or more, the water pushing up to the edge of the marsh grass and into the higher ground behind it.

When the marsh is flooded, the water within the grass shimmers with the movement of schools of small fish and shellfish among the stalks, comfortable within the shelter of the marsh, which hides them from predators in the channels and at the grass's edge. The stalks and roots are covered with algae and other microscopic organisms that provide nurture for slightly larger organisms higher up the food chain. Snails climb Spartina stalks to escape the water and fiddlers and other crabs scurry to higher ground, clicking as they move.

From a kayak one views the marsh at water level, submerged within the grass. As you paddle along a marsh channel, white shrimp jump before you and finger mullet skitter into the flooded grass. Around a corner you encounter an ibis feeding at the marsh edge, its curved scarlet beak probing deep into the muck for worms and crabs, plunging deeper, searching with the nerves on the tip of the beak, pulling back and searching again, watching you out of the corner of a wary eye.

The marsh is a quiet place, so quiet that even small sounds reach a paddler. As you ease along, the loud aaark of a heron from somewhere within the grass may startle you. As you glide into the open water of a marsh pond, a flock of resting wigeon at the far end may take flight, a flurry of ducks rising sharply and then banking back over you to land in an adjacent pond. Ahead in the water you see the moving vee that is the wake of a large fish, perhaps a redfish. This is a living ecosystem and you are immersed within it.

By car, one can get close to some of the salt marshes along the inland side of barrier islands. Among the more accessible places for kayakers are East Bay marshes on the bay side of the Bolivar Peninsula, between the ferry to Galveston and High Island (try launching at Stingaree Marina); West Bay marshes along the bay shore of Galveston Island (try launching at Galveston Island State Park); Christmas and Drum Bay marshes on the bay side of Folletts Island, between San Luis Pass and Freeport; and the Lower Colorado River Authority park at the mouth of the Colorado River at Matagorda. Galveston Island State Park also has an excellent boardwalk reaching into the marsh, where those not inclined to paddle can get a closer look.

Prior to the twentieth century, much greater areas of freshwater marsh existed in the region than are found today. Freshwater marsh requires large amounts of rainfall to ward off the salinity that is ever-present on the coast. Historically, rainfall runoff moved from the slightly higher prairie uplands downward into the lower-lying lands of the marsh system, moving toward sea level and the Gulf in an overland flow pattern. In this manner, the marshes grade from the freshest areas adjacent to the prairies to the saltiest marsh adjacent to the bay.

Today, classic fresh marsh is declining, primarily due to drainage alterations. The Gulf Intracoastal Waterway is a man-made channel traversing the

length of the Texas coast and connecting our various bay systems. Between the bays, this canal cuts through the marshlands, interrupting the north-to-south overland flow regime and providing a pathway for saltier water to move from the bays into the adjacent fresher marshes. Additionally, various other channels have been constructed to support oil and gas operations and other uses, adding to the movement of saltier water into the fresh marsh. The net result is that we are losing fresh marsh.

Intermediate or brackish marsh has a greater ability to withstand salt and is not as disadvantaged by this increase in salinity as is the fresh marsh. By definition, the intermediate marsh stands between fresh and salt. In exchange for being more salt tolerant, the number of plant species that can tolerate this environment declines. Although the intermediate marsh does not have quite the species diversity of a fresh marsh, it is nevertheless a valuable resource for waterfowl coming south down the central flyway of the United States. Salt tolerance is important on the coast. Storms regularly bring surge tides of eight to ten feet that flood all of the marsh, and even the freshwater marsh can absorb a blow that comes only once every decade or so.

However, when salt is present day in and day out, it kills the plants. After the plants die, their roots slough off along with the soil holding the root masses, and the marsh becomes an open body of water, lacking the food and habitat it once provided. All along the coast, there is growing concern about rising sea level and the impacts that a sea level rise could have on the long-term viability of the intermediate and fresh marshes.

Fresh marsh can be found on the western side of Sabine Lake, extending across the southern portions of Jefferson County, and extensive areas of brackish marsh have been preserved. From a national perspective, these areas are sufficiently important to migratory waterfowl for the scarce monies for land

purchase to have been provided by both the federal and state governments to ensure conservation of large areas of fresh and intermediate marshes. We can thank Congress and the Texas Legislature for what is already preserved, while still working to set aside more of the remaining tracts.

At winter's dawn, the intermediate marsh is alive with ducks and their sounds, the whistles of the wigeon and pintail, the quack of the gadwall and the mottled duck. In a year with good rainfall, the marsh is full of good food for ducks, foodstuffs such as wigeon grass and wild celery. The ducks that frequent the fresh and intermediate marshes are dabbling ducks, rather than diving ducks found in the bays. A dabbling duck feeds by tipping its tail up and reaching down toward the pond's bottom with its long neck. It is common to see duck rumps raised to the sky, a sign of great feeding on the pond or flooded flat.

One fine intermediate marsh is owned by the Brown Foundation, a Houston charitable organization. January of 2006 found these brackish marshlands very dry, with retreating water levels due to a dry fall. Water was standing only at the lowest elevations, in a series of ponds that were in heavy demand by ducks and other waterfowl due to the season's reduced freshwater marsh habitat all along the coast.

Looking into the brackish marsh along the shoreline of East Bay, Jim Neville, a former staffer with U.S. Fish and Wildlife Service, described its value. Jim can differentiate the grass species at a glance, noting subtleties that escape the eye of those of us who are not experts. Among his projects is monitoring the creation of ponds for mottled ducks that nest in the Houston Wilderness.

Jim pointed to an area covered by black rush, one of the major food sources in the marsh. The white heads of snow geese could be seen among the green stalks of the rushes. At another location, Jim pointed out an area where the land was churned up and the roots of plants were clearly visible. This was what is known as an "eat out," a place where geese have taken over a portion of the marsh and eaten out the vegetation. During the early fall, the marsh is often burned so that new grass can sprout.

One of the best places to get to know both fresh and intermediate marsh is the Anahuac National Wildlife Refuge. Roads allow visitors to observe the marsh from a car, including on a loop drive around Shovelers Pond, which has a viewing deck and a boardwalk reaching into the marsh. This section of the refuge has deeper freshwater channels, some open water, and adjacent areas that are covered with vegetation. In a wet year, the entire area is flooded, while in a dry year the standing water covers only portions of it.

As you drive along the edge of this large wetland, a small, ducklike bird may be swimming in the channel and then diving, only to reappear fifty feet farther down: a grebe, fishing. A larger bird—a dramatic, brilliant rainbow of purple and aquamarine, with a yellow and red bill—is supported on long toes as it proceeds among the marsh plants and over the lily pads: a purple gallinule is out foraging. This species nests in the area after spending the winter in Central and South America.

At Anahuac on a sunny day, you will see lots of alligators. Alligators are cold-blooded, relying upon the sunlight to provide body heat. In the late spring, there may be several alligators in view from the Shovelers Pond loop. Alligators were endangered for a time but rebounded fast during two decades when hunting and trapping seasons were closed; their egg clutches are large. They are now relatively abundant once more, and hunting has resumed.

The mud along the edges of the deeper channel is smoothed down where gators slide in and out of the water. The marsh hay cordgrass, Spartina patens, is flattened where the gators have been basking. A large

gator lying in the sun is an impressive sight—six to seven feet or more of glistening gray-black skin, a bony head with extruding eyes, and a prehistoric mouth full of teeth that glint in the sunlight. Small gators may seem appealing, but there is no mistaking the seriousness of an adult alligator.

Along the Shovelers Pond driving loop and boardwalk it is also possible to get quite close to birds that are usually difficult to see. During the fall and winter, the waters are filled with ducks and other waterfowl of every description. Among those readily identified is the northern shoveler drake with its white and orange-brown breast, bright green head, and spoon-shaped bill—the bird is affectionately known as a "spoonie." The blue-winged teal drake has a striking pale half moon across its blue-gray head, and the green-winged teal drake has a resplendent emerald green patch behind the eye.

Among the more visible of the freshwater bird species are the coots and moorhens that frequent the channels adjacent to the auto trail. The coots are black with white bills and paddle along in small groups, often within the thick vegetation. When spooked, they seem to run across the water's surface, their wings flapping but their feet doing most of the work. The moorhens look similar, but have orange bills and are more brown than they are black.

If you are lucky, a secretive bird may move a few steps out of the marsh grass onto the mud bank of the channel, then slip quickly back into the screening vegetation. Had you not seen it, you would have no idea it was there. The grass does not move as the bird slips between the stalks. You have seen a rail, and it could be any of the several species that frequent our marshes—a clapper rail, king rail or the smaller yellow rail. The expression "thin as a rail" has bearing: the birds' bodies are laterally compressed for creeping among reeds and grasses. Perhaps you will get a better look next time.

Around the turn, a brown animal that looks like a large rat moves slowly along the marsh edge. This is a nutria, an imported species that has found a home in the marshes of southeast Texas. For many years the nutria population grew fast, and the animals were damaging the marsh. However, as the alligators increased under the protection of the federal Endangered Species Act, nutria numbers have been checked by these top predators

Historically, the marsh was also full of other furbearers, notably otters and muskrats. These animals still can be found, but they are much less common than they used to be. Predators such as bobcats roam the marsh, as do coyotes. The red wolf that formerly frequented this area is no longer found in the wild on the Texas coast, although red wolf-coyote hybrids may persist. This wolf species was once common all throughout the southeastern United States, but populations were severely reduced during the era of government-supported predator control. The last of the wild red wolves were trapped in this part of Texas and adjacent Louisiana and transported to a federal reserve in the Carolinas, where they became the nucleus of a successful captive breeding and recovery program. Experimental populations have now been introduced in three other wildlife refuges.

Leaving the Anahuac National Wildlife Refuge on a later winter afternoon, with the sun softly shining on the marsh hay, you may watch a flight of snow geese moving gracefully across the sky. These geese winter on the upper Texas coast and breed in the far north of Canada, inextricably linking our region to the great wilderness expanses of James Bay and the Arctic Circle. Suddenly the geese tumble from the sky, wings folded in, bodies dipping as they drop downward, wings extending only at the last moment to break the fall and catch the air as the birds glide to the ground and join more than a thousand other snows in the safety of the marsh grass, protected within the refuge.

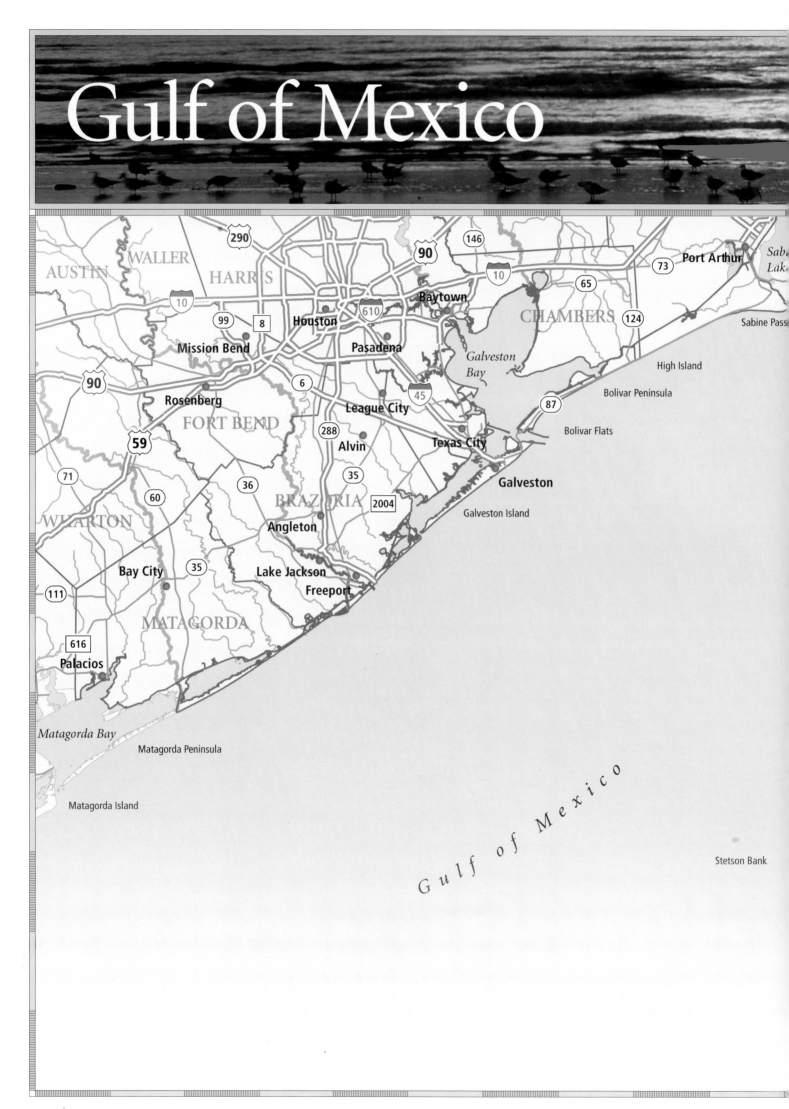

# Gulf of Mexico

## THE FLOWER GARDEN

East Flower Garden

West Flower Garden

Gulf of Mexico

State Parks, WMA's and
National Wildlife Refuges

**THE HOUSTON WILDERNESS AREA** is bordered on the southeast by the vast ecosystem of the Gulf of Mexico. Most of us come in contact with this ecosystem when we visit our barrier islands and beaches—sandy lands that are formed by the interaction of the Gulf currents, river runoff and the mainland.

The beaches of the upper Texas coast are a mixture of sand and silt, flanked by sand dunes and associated wetlands on the landward side and water on the other side. These beaches are popular swimming, surfing and loafing areas for coastal residents during much of the year. Among our more popular beaches are the Bolivar Peninsula, Galveston Island, Surfside on Follet's Island in Brazoria County, and Matagorda at the mouth of the Colorado River.

When we come to the beach to play, few of us realize that we are entering an ecosystem that connects the Texas coast to Florida and Mexico, the Caribbean Sea and the Atlantic Ocean. Except at the edges, humans are not part of this system unless they have an artificial support system such as a boat or an offshore oil rig. This is an ecosystem of marine mammals and deepwater fishes, of whales and dolphins and sharks and red snapper and the millions of smaller fish upon which they feed.

*A newly hatched Kemp's Ridley sea turtle makes its way toward the gulf waters.*

0    2.5    5    10    15    20 miles

*Species of the beaches and gulf waters from top left to right: Common nighthawk,* Chordeiles minor*; Bottlenose dolphin,* Tursiops truncates*; Great egret,* Ardea alba. *Evening primrose,* Oenothera macrocarpa, *grows on beach dunes, helping to stabilize and enlarge the dune. Larger dunes help protect the land and homes behind the dune from storm surge and slow down the effects of erosion.*

The waves roll in across the Gulf, pushed by the predominant southeast winds, in toward the beach. Each wave spends itself against gravity as it pushes up the inclining beach slope, leaving fluffy white foam at the uppermost edge. Here the shorebirds feed, dashing down with the retreating wave, running back as the next comes in, plucking tiny morsels from the sand and foam.

As you walk into the surf, the water gets deeper, covering your ankles and then your knees. If you look carefully, you may see small fish and possibly a crab in the shallow trough. If you reach down and pull up a handful of sand, you may find any number of small shells that are home to organisms living in the benthic zone—the bottom beneath the water. Often the beach is filled with larger shells that are washed in after a storm, usually after the organism living inside has died.

As you walk further into the surf, you encounter a shallower zone, a sand bar that is marked by breaking waves. As you walk off the other side of the sand bar, the water quickly becomes much deeper, coming up to your waist or even higher. You are startled by a jumping mullet, a common smaller fish that is the food of many larger fish species, a reminder that you are within a living system.

Ahead, the white foam from the larger breakers on the next sand bar are clearly visible, a place of high energy and turbulent water. It is here that you can body-surf by thrusting your body in a prone position before an oncoming wave, letting the force of the breaking wave carry you forward on a thrilling ride.

Like the beach itself, the sand bars are shaped by the physical forces of water meeting land. Five thousand years ago the Gulf of Mexico was several hundred feet lower in elevation, meaning that water met land more than one hundred miles farther out than today. As sea level rose with the retreat of the glaciers, sediment flowing from the rivers and sand deposits resuspended by the rising water were deposited where water and land met. In this manner, the barrier islands and sand bars were formed.

Another factor involved in the formation of the beach and bars is the longshore drift. If you play in the waves for a while, you may notice that you have moved southward over time, particularly if you are on a raft or some type of float. This movement to the south is due to the longshore drift, a current that always moves from the upper Texas coast southward toward Padre Island, where it meets a current coming from the opposite direction. This is simply a physical fact of the Gulf on the upper Texas coast.

The longshore drift has helped form one of the best birdwatching places in the world on our upper Texas coast—the Bolivar Flats. When the Houston Ship Channel was deepened to allow large ships to come into Galveston Bay, rock barriers called jetties were built on either side of the deep channel cutting into the Gulf of Mexico to prevent the channel from being filled with silt. The north jetty—the one on the Bolivar Peninsula—traps tremendous amounts of silt that is moving from north to south with the longshore current. In this manner, a large area has been transformed to fabulous habitat for all types of wading and fish-eating birds.

On a typical outing to the Bolivar Flats one can see thousands, if not hundreds of thousands, of birds. There may be avocets—medium-sized wading birds with an upturned bill, a black and white body, and a light-brown head—or the black and white stilt with its long pink legs. A raft of white pelicans may be floating or fishing together. Reddish egrets can be seen fishing with their wings spread, dancing across the flats next to hundreds of small waders—dowitchers and sanderlings and plovers—huddled together on the exposed sand.

Birdwatchers come from across the world to see the Bolivar Flats, an area that has been preserved by the Houston Audubon Society. This is one of

*Species of the Flower Garden Banks include from left to right: Queen parrotfish,* Scarus vetula; *Jackknife fish,* Equetus lanceolatus; *Atlantic Deer cowrie,* Cypraea cervus; *branching fire coral,* Millepora alcicornis, *with orange elephant ear sponge,* Agelas clathrodes *and brown chromis,* Chromis multilineata.

the most accessible areas to see a great variety of shorebirds and waders, as well as various ducks. The flats are just a short ferry ride from the city of Galveston and can easily be visited in an afternoon from most of the Houston Wilderness area.

The barrier islands and beaches that form the landward side of the Gulf are unique sand systems. These are active geological areas that can be changed quickly by tropical storms and hurricanes coming in from the Gulf. And make no mistake about it—the Gulf is a weather maker as well as an ecosystem. In the summer, all residents of the upper Texas coast keep their eyes on the weather maps, hoping that the next tropical storm or hurricane will not come ashore here.

Over the years, these sandy barrier islands have been hit hard by storms, with the proof being any number of deep channels cut into the landward side of these barrier islands. These channels are now fringed with marshes and provide excellent habitat on the bay side of the islands, places full of juvenile shrimp and fish-eating birds. However, they were formed—literally blown open—by the force of the storms coming in from the Gulf.

On a barrier island there is a normal progression of landforms, from the sandy beach to the wispy, vegetation-covered sand dunes, to freshwater wetlands lacing the prairies behind the dunes, and brackish and salt marsh lining the bay side of the island. Some of the best birdwatching on the coast can be found on Stewart Road, a back road leading from the city of Galveston to the west end of the island and San Luis Pass, the natural connection between West Bay and Christmas Bay and the Gulf of Mexico.

The Gulf is an important natural system that is connected to our bays and is also connected to the Caribbean Sea and the Atlantic Ocean. The Gulf is the ninth-largest water body in the world with some 3,400 miles of shoreline and covering approximately 940,000 square miles (1.5 million square kilometers). The continental slope provides a shallow shelf off the upper Texas coast, requiring a trip of more than sixty miles offshore to find water more than a hundred feet deep. Farther out, the deepest waters of the Gulf extend deeper than 9,000 feet.

The fisheries are fantastic, with over 1.7 billion pounds of fish and shellfish brought ashore in the five states bordering the Gulf. Biologists have counted more than three hundred species of fish off the Texas shore. There are deep-sea marine mammals such as the pantropical spotted dolphin, sperm whales, the dwarf or pygmy sperm whale, Risso's dolphin, bottlenose dolphin and rough-toothed dolphin. Of these, only the bottlenose dolphin can be commonly seen close to land.

The Gulf is a water ecosystem full of living organisms. In the nearshore area are smaller fish and game fish such as speckled trout and red drum and croaker, a fact revealed by the groups of fishermen wading in the surf and standing on the wooden Gulf fishing piers. When clear water moves in from offshore, pelagic fish species like Spanish and king mackerel move in toward the beach. Schools of tarpon range within sight of the beach during the summer, as do a wide variety of sharks that basically are uninterested in humans.

Both brown and white shrimp use the estuaries as nurseries and migrate to the Gulf when they mature. In the Gulf, these shrimp breed, lay their eggs, and then die, usually at an age of only fifteen months or so. Often during the summer and fall, shrimp boats can be seen pulling their nets near the beach, trying to catch the shrimp that are moving further out in the Gulf to breed. Shrimping is highly regulated and controversial, yet it is part of our coastal heritage.

One of the most important fishery management issues in the Gulf of Mexico involves management

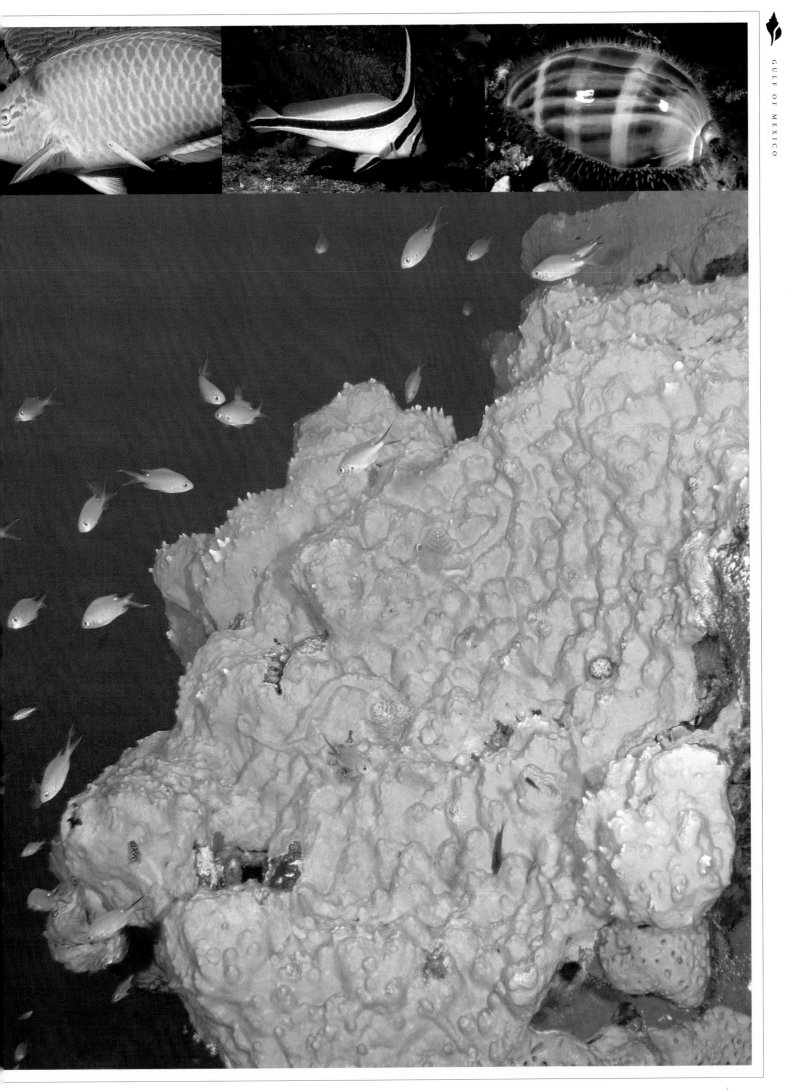

Bottom right: Endangered
Least terns, Sterna antillarum,
use the Gulf beaches as
breeding grounds and spend
2-3 weeks in a noisy courtship
that usually includes a "fish
flight" - an aerial display

involving aerobatics and
pursuit, ending in a fish
transfer on the ground
between two displaying birds.

of the red snapper. Red snapper live in the deeper water on the continental shelf and are valued for their tasty white meat. They live in large schools and can be overfished with modern commercial as well as recreational fishing techniques and technology. Young red snapper can also be caught in shrimp nets and killed as "bycatch" of the shrimping process, as can sea turtles.

As a result of these potential impacts, fisheries in the Gulf are managed extensively. The red snapper catch—both commercial and recreational—is controlled by the Gulf of Mexico Fishery Management Council, whereas the potential impacts to turtles are controlled under the U.S. Endangered Species Act. Today, shrimp nets have turtle-excluder devices and bycatch reduction devices—holes in the net—to reduce the impact of shrimping. By the same token, tight regulations govern both commercial and recreational take of red snapper.

Although the fisheries of the Gulf are bountiful, they are not without limits. It is extremely difficult to analyze and understand fish populations and how much fish can be harvested without harming the overall population. Obviously, if too many are taken, the population can be jeopardized.

To date, we have been fortunate along the Gulf of Mexico in that we have not seen the severe impacts to our fisheries that have occurred, for example, with cod in the northeastern United States. Many of us enjoy eating shrimp or red snapper at local seafood restaurants and often take for granted that these fish and shellfish resources will be here for us to enjoy. The next time you order red snapper, you might thank the Gulf of Mexico Fishery Management Council for making sure that we continue to have a breeding population that will keep red snapper in the Gulf.

One of the biggest surprises offshore of Freeport in the southern portion of the Houston Wilderness area is the presence of coral reefs that compare with those of the Caribbean Sea. This area is known as the Flower Garden and was designated a marine sanctuary in 1992. The Flower Garden consists of the East Flower Garden Bank, the West Flower Garden Bank and the Stetson Bank, and they represent a unique ecological resource.

These coral reefs grow atop salt domes—geological formations that push up the soil and sediment above them. These domes rise to within sixty to seventy feet of the water surface and were named by sailors who could see the beautiful coral formations down through the clear Gulf water—like a flower garden underwater.

The reefs are true Caribbean coral, probably brought in by the prevailing currents. There are twenty-one species of coral in the sanctuary. There are more than eighty species of algae, two hundred and fifty species of macroinvertebrates, and more than two hundred species of fish, including many of the colorful reef species, as well as three kinds of marine turtles.

The Stetson Bank is the closest of the reserves to shore, being about seventy miles south of Galveston. Both the East and West Flower Gardens are an additional thirty or so miles out. Together, these reserves represent about four hundred acres of reef crest and about forty-three square miles of reserve that are enjoyed by scuba divers traveling out of Freeport and Galveston.

Back on the beach, a flock of brown pelicans flies over the breakers, rising with the crest of the wave, and lowering again to skim close over the water. Every so often, a pelican rises and then plunges beak-first into the water, catching its dinner.

Brown pelicans were once prevalent on the upper Texas coast, and then they disappeared, victims of pesticides that caused their eggs to weaken and break. Today, the brown pelican is back again, a testament to our ability to reverse ecological harm with our science and a will to protect living things.

# Bayou Wilderness

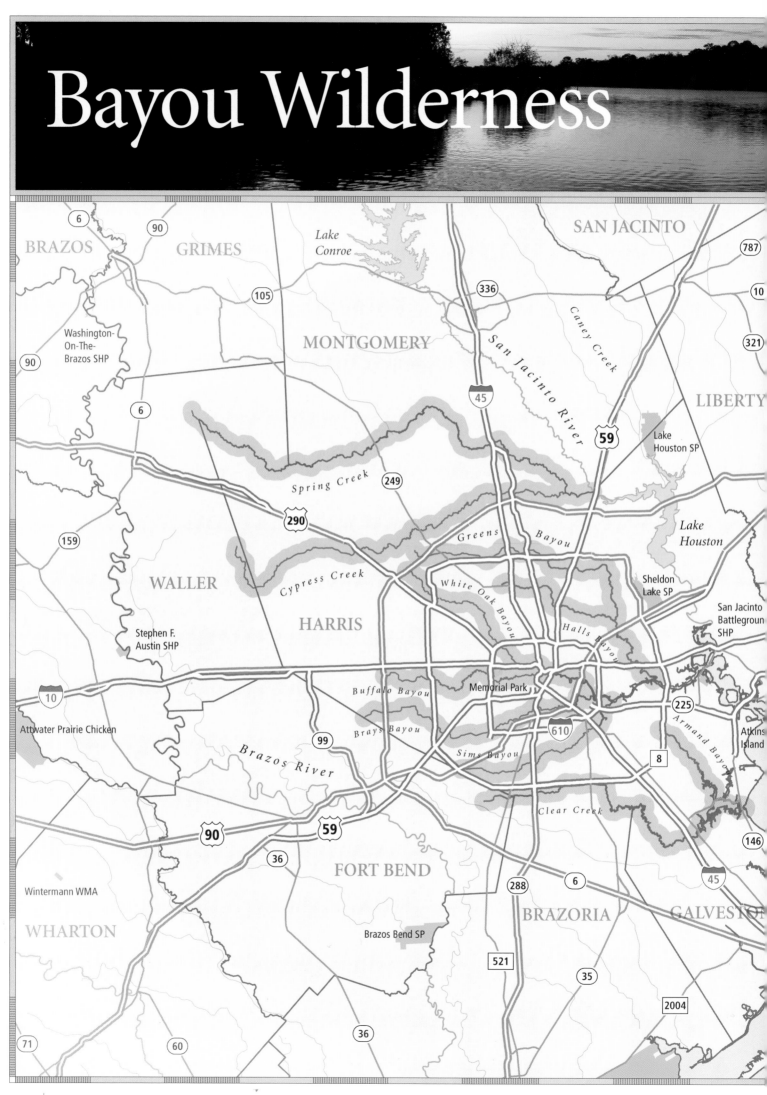

River NWR

Davis Hill SNA

HARDIN

River NWR

(326)

(146)

(105)

*Trinity River*

(90)

(61)

ty River NWR

0

(65)

CHAMBERS

(124)

Anahuac

eston

Moody

Candy Abshier WMA

Rollover
Fish Pass

(87)

Houston Bayous

State Parks, WMA's and
National Wildlife Refuges

eston
d SP

**WE HAVE GOOD REASON** to call Houston the Bayou City. It is crisscrossed by waterways of all types, cutting through the flat coastal plain. We have rivers, bayous and creeks, some coming in from afar, some rising in the Houston Wilderness and flowing into the estuaries or directly to the Gulf, and some flowing through highly developed portions of Harris County. This chapter is a tribute to the bayou wilderness that still exists within the greater Houston metropolitan area.

Harris County and Houston are bisected by Buffalo Bayou, which rises in the Katy Prairie west of the city and flows to the east through the Memorial area and right through downtown, its course eventually becoming the deepwater Houston Ship Channel.

Buffalo Bayou is joined by several other bayous that define various Houston neighborhoods. Its northern tributaries include White Oak Bayou, flowing in from northwest Harris County through the Houston Heights and emptying into Buffalo Bayou downtown. Hunting Bayou is a small waterway entering the Houston Ship Channel near East Loop 610. South of Bush Intercontinental Airport, Greens Bayou flows eastward near Beltway 8 , and then turns south, again paralleling the beltway, where it is joined by

*Experiencing a quiet morning on Armand Bayou. Even within the city limits, there are pockets of wilderness to enjoy where people can forget they are within a thriving metropolis.*

0     2.5     5          10          15       20 miles

Halls Bayou on its way to the Houston Ship Channel. On the south side of the city, Brays Bayou flows from the southwest through the Houston Medical Center to join Buffalo Bayou east of downtown. Sims Bayou also drains southern Harris County, flowing through the Hobby Airport area to enter the deepwater Buffalo Bayou east of the Brays Bayou inflow.

Other natural watercourses in greater Houston are Cypress Creek and Spring Creek, which flow across northern Harris County to join the San Jacinto River in forming Lake Houston. Spring Creek forms the boundary between Harris and Montgomery counties, while Cypress Creek rises in Waller County and flows through the Katy Prairie. Both these creeks are bordered by pine forests with adjacent hardwoods and massive white sand bars, the appealing terrain of the FM 1960 area, Spring and the Woodlands.

To the south, Clear Creek flows from Brazoria County eastward to Galveston Bay, forming the boundary between Harris and Galveston counties. As it moves toward the bay, Clear Creek becomes Clear Lake, the setting now famous for NASA's Johnson Space Center, the home of the manned space flight program. The Clear Creek watershed also includes Armand Bayou, flowing into Clear Lake. Portions of the shores of Clear Creek and Clear Lake lie in Houston, Pasadena and a series of smaller communities—League City, Clear Lake Shores, Kemah, Seabrook, Taylor Lake Village, El Lago, Webster, Nassau Bay and Friendswood.

The size of the smaller creeks and bayous is misleading. These waterways are characterized by a relatively small incised channel that is cut into the clay of the flat coastal plain. Most of the time water flows in this cut channel. On some bayous the channel may be as small as ten to fifteen feet in width and only a few feet deep, while others are wider and deeper. The important point, however, is that the incised channels were formed over thousands of years and carry only the low to average flows. When big rains come, the creeks and bayous simply rise out of their banks and spread out to cover whatever land is necessary to accommodate the water.

And big rains do come to the Houston area. It is common for rainfall amounts of three to four inches to fall over a twelve-hour period. Our so-called one-hundred-year rainfall event—(rainfall intensity sufficiently rare that it occurs only once every one hundred years)—is estimated to be just over thirteen inches in a twenty-four-hour period. But we have had several measured events in which the rainfall exceeded twenty inches over a twenty-four-hour period. During Tropical Storm Allison in June 2001, a station in northeast Houston recorded more than twenty-six inches of rain in less than ten hours. Tropical Storm Claudette in July 1979 dropped forty-two inches of rain in northern Brazoria County in twenty-four hours. Big rains do indeed occur.

Looking carefully at natural streams and bayous, one can usually identify a relatively flat area adjacent to the incised channel, with a greater rise in the land surface elevation beyond this, farther

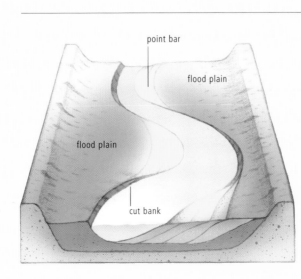

*Anatomy of a Meandering Bayou. The water current is constantly eroding the outer bend, which creates a cut bank, and carrying sediment and depositing it further downstream on the next inside bend, which creates a point bar.*

*Species of the Bayou Wilderness ecoregion include from top left to right: Great blue heron,* Ardea herodias; *Wood duck,* Aix sponsa; *Orchard Orbweaver,* Leucauge venusta, *and the migratory Monarch,* Danaus plexippus.

away from the channel. This is the secondary channel that carries water during larger storms. It is called the floodplain of a stream or bayou. In its natural condition the floodplain is the site of great biological diversity, including varied hardwood trees and shrubs as well as a great diversity of mammals, birds, reptiles and amphibians.

This floodplain is part of the bayou. It functions as a flow zone during larger storm events, serving as an area that the bayou uses only part of the time. We can be sure that from time to time the floodwater will expand from the channel into this area. Our legal system, however, has failed to acknowledge that floodplains are part of the natural streams. Instead of setting aside the floodplain as a part of the watercourse, we have divided it up and allowed it to be sold for development. At best, this is extremely hazardous. Floodplain areas are bound to flood, and to flood repeatedly. They are part of the bayou, not part of the upland.

As Houston developed, housing and commercial structures were built adjacent to the bayous. In some cases structures were built close to the water for navigation and trade reasons. In other cases people wanted to be close to the water for the natural beauty. Predictably, these structures often flooded, and the flooding led to physical modifications of some watercourses in an attempt to reduce flood damage.

Some waterways were widened and deepened and lined with concrete, virtually eliminating their biological diversity; examples are Brays and White Oak bayous. Others, such as Buffalo Bayou east of downtown, were widened and deepened to provide deepwater navigation, removing the natural cypress stands and hardwoods. However, some creeks and bayous have escaped extensive modification and exist today in their natural state, offering respite from the surrounding city.

West of downtown, Buffalo Bayou is a ribbon of life extending through urbanized Houston. This stretch of Buffalo Bayou was once the focus of a channelizing proposal that would have destroyed it but was saved by the intervention of the forty-first president of the United States, George H. W. Bush, when he was still a congressman, and by Terry Hershey, Houston's environmental godmother. Today, it is simply an urban marvel.

Don Greene has been taking people on canoe trips down Buffalo Bayou for more than two decades. Through those many years, he has never lost his enthusiasm for the place or the trip. Don has great appreciation for the subtleties of the natural bayou, for how the stream flow creates eddy pools, for how the bank is eroded on the outer side of a bayou turn and how the land "accretes" on the inside of the turn. Don reads the water like most people read books.

A trip normally starts where West Loop 610 crosses Buffalo Bayou. Here, you put in at a shallow backwater and paddle out into the surprisingly fast flow of Buffalo Bayou. You have to watch for the pilings on the 610 bridge and avoid "strainers" where the current flows through downed trees. These strainers provide excellent aquatic habitat and are often perching sites for fish-eating birds such as the belted kingfisher and great egret. Strainers are also hazards to the unsuspecting canoeist. The current is stronger than you might think and can easily tip a canoe pushed against a downed tree. Everyone should be wearing a life jacket.

As you move down the bayou, city life slips away from your consciousness. The concrete and steel of freeway bridges and adjacent buildings transition to towering pines and oaks with an understory of yaupon and beautyberry. The noise so noticeable at the bridge fades away; soon the bayou is a quiet stream within a mixed pine-hardwood forest.

The elements of the natural bayou swim into focus. The banks are cut through clay and mud, with various layers clearly visible just above the water's edge. Certain layers appear to be weeping as groundwater seeps from a sandier zone above an impermeable clay layer; the groundwater moves slowly along within the more permeable layer and emerges where it can. After heavy rains the subsoil drains for weeks, slowly releasing into the bayou the rainwater stored during the storm.

A small sand bar at the water's edge shows a jumble of footprints. Side-by-side tracks with four long digits indicate the presence of a raccoon at the edge, probably washing off dinner. Farther down, the sand reveals the spread three-toed footprints of several large birds, the remains of a crayfish testifying that some predator was here. Butterflies flicker in the dappled sunlight falling on the bayou through the forest. Two sulphur yellow butterflies land on the sand bar and take water. Several orange and black butterflies flit among the flowering shrubs on the bank, along with numerous honeybees and bumblebees.

Pulling to the bank and walking quietly into the forest, you may catch a glimpse of the source of rustling in the leaves up on the floodplain bench. The animal taking itself out of sight is most likely an armadillo. Welcome to the bayou shore of Memorial Park and its floodplain forest, complete with large oaks reaching far above the yaupon and beautyberry understory.

Back in the canoe and rounding a bend brings you to another tree that has fallen in the water. A diamond-backed water snake glides gracefully away from the floating branches and from the paddlers steering around the obstruction. A fish rolls on the surface of the bayou, offering a passing glance at the prehistoric-looking alligator gar. A squeal may signal a pair of wood ducks taking off from a pool not yet in view. And all around are

the sounds of the woodland birds—the harsh cry of blue jay, the soft trill of the chickadee, the sweet inquiry of the cardinal and the piercing call of a pileated woodpecker emerging from the top of the floodplain forest, a dash of red and black in the blue sky between the emerald green trees.

A trip down Buffalo Bayou also provides testament to the power of the floods. One sees example after example of the failure of structures intended to control the natural force of the water—steel sheet piling pushed outward by the force of groundwater movement from soils saturated with floodwater, along with concrete mats and sheets collapsing into the water. While these streams look small, they become incredibly powerful when carrying the floodwater runoff of heavy storms.

Nearing the Shepherd Drive bridge, paddlers become aware of the city once again. Condominiums appear on the north side of the bayou, houses on the south. Continuing down the bayou takes you floating into downtown Houston, where glass-sheathed buildings scrape the sky in mind-bending contrast to the natural vistas of earlier in the day.

To enjoy the same habitats on foot, the Houston Arboretum offers an excellent trail system through the floodplain forest to the edge of Buffalo Bayou. Many of the trees and shrubs are marked, which reveals their impressive variety. The arboretum has identified one hundred and two species of trees and shrubs within its one hundred and fifty-acre tract, and most are signed and located on maps. The arboretum has a bird list with more than one hundred and sixty-five species that can be seen on the property at various times of the year; thirty-one mammals, including bobcat and numerous bats; thirteen amphibians, twenty-seven reptiles, and twenty-two varieties of fish.

The bayou is full of life because food, cover and water are found here in a space largely without a

human presence. A fine time for a trip down the bayou is in spring, when the hardwoods put out their new leaves and the forest is painted in varying tones of fresh green; but any time on the bayou is a good time.

Clear Creek and Armand Bayou in southern Harris County provide a similar experience. Clear Creek rises in eastern Brazoria County and flows eastward through Pearland and Friendswood to League City, where it becomes the tidal estuary called Clear Lake. Armand Bayou flows southward from Pasadena to enter Clear Lake near the Johnson Space Center. However, unlike the natural portion of Buffalo Bayou, the lower courses of Clear Creek and Armand Bayou contain tidal wetlands as well as floodplain forests. The coastal habitat means that these waterways contain a greater diversity of fish and shellfish, including crabs and shrimp as well as a greater abundance of fish-eating birds such as the osprey, great egrets and even the reddish egret.

The preservation of bayous and creeks has been a long-standing interest for some Houston citizens. Their focused effort has resulted in purchase of open space adjacent to creeks and bayous to be set aside for public use. In this manner, many important lands have been preserved, including several tracts on Spring and Cypress creeks, Greens Bayou, Clear Creek and Armand Bayou. Today, these parklands are being connected by a series of trails that will allow much greater access to and appreciation of the bayou wilderness.

An exciting proposition is the attempt to restore bayous transformed in the past by channelization. Along both Brays and White Oak bayous are large developed areas that continue to flood despite the lining of the bayous with concrete. The continued flooding problems reveal an earlier lack of understanding of the hydrologic function of the prairies, which used to hold massive amounts of rainwater in wetland potholes and flats as well as in rice fields.

As prairies to the west of Houston have been developed, the hydrologic regime has changed. Prior to development, rainfall was stored in the prairie wetlands, slowly running off into creeks and bayous over many days and weeks. After development, storm sewers and concrete drainage ditches push the storm water into the bayous and creeks much faster than under natural conditions, increasing the peak flows by a factor of five or even ten when compared to the original flows. This phenomenon was first recognized in the 1970s and is now well defined in the scientific literature.

The bottom line is that our earlier efforts to control flooding could not provide protection against the huge volumes of water dumped from upstream development, and our flooding problems persist. New policies have now begun to emphasize buying out flood-prone properties and removing the vulnerable homes. As we remove homes from flood-prone areas, opportunities arise for habitat enhancement even along channelized watercourses. In some places the stream courses can be widened to create wetlands. The forest can be reestablished on the bench above the incised channel. In short, to some degree we can allow the floodplains to return; there is no need for these places to remain biologically impoverished.

There is thus much to celebrate in our bayou wilderness. We have areas that have managed to emerge into the twenty-first century relatively intact and others that need to be rehabilitated. Trail systems connecting them will form a web reaching upstream from developed areas into the prairies and pine forests, and downstream to the estuaries and marshes, linking city dwellers of every species along the waterways to our rural surroundings, connecting us all to our wilderness.

# Protected Lands

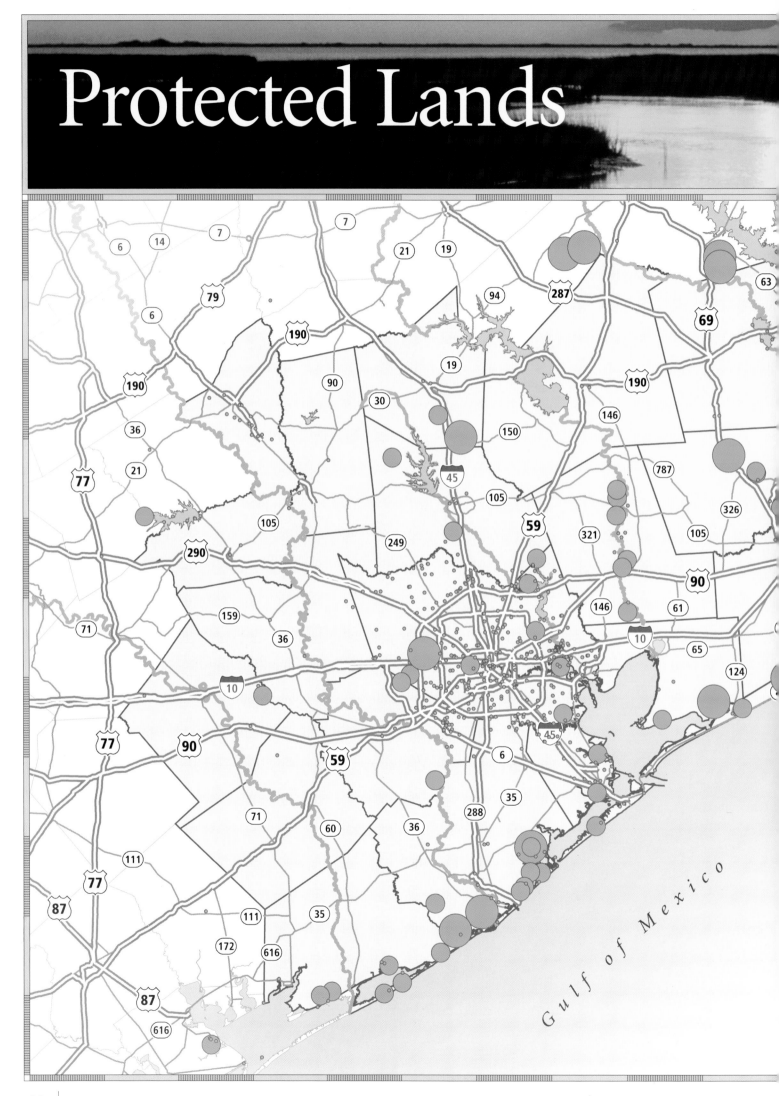

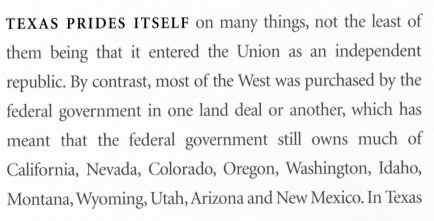

**TEXAS PRIDES ITSELF** on many things, not the least of them being that it entered the Union as an independent republic. By contrast, most of the West was purchased by the federal government in one land deal or another, which has meant that the federal government still owns much of California, Nevada, Colorado, Oregon, Washington, Idaho, Montana, Wyoming, Utah, Arizona and New Mexico. In Texas nearly all the land is in the hands of private owners.

The lack of extensive land ownership by either the federal or state government means that if we are to protect our biological diversity by protecting lands, we must purchase, acquire conservation easements, or otherwise set aside these lands. Those who want lands protected must find the money from public and private sources to protect important wildlife and recreational areas.

Over the years, stretches of important habitat have indeed been set aside. However, the value of some of our ecological resources is only now being recognized, and as a region we are still playing catch-up to conserve meaningful acreages. Today, when competition for federal, state and private dollars is immense, one major goal for the Houston Wilderness area is to bring in substantial financial capital to protect our most important natural capital. It is a testament to the importance of our nat-

*The Republic of Texas seal represented the independent country that existed from 1836 to 1845.*

< 1000 acres

1000 - 10,000 acres

> 10,000 acres

*Parks under 25 acres omitted*

0    10    20         40 miles

*Scenes from Texas' protected lands from top left to right: Dunes at Matagorda; an Armadillo,* Dasypus novemcinctus, *at Martin Dies Jr. State Park; an Attwater's prairie-chicken,* Tympanuchus cupido attwateri *on the Attwater Prairie Chicken National Wildlife Refuge.*

ural capital on a national level that money is coming into the region today even when land purchase budgets are extremely small.

The federal government has invested heavily in the region over the years and continues to do so. Most of the important marshlands between Sabine Lake and Galveston Bay are part of the national wildlife refuge system, including the Texas Point, McFaddin, Anahuac and Moody national wildlife refuges. On the north side of West Bay is the Brazoria National Wildlife Refuge, followed down the coast by the San Bernard, Big Boggy and Matagorda national wildlife refuges. More recently, the U.S. Fish and Wildlife Service has started purchasing bottomland tracts for the Trinity River National Wildlife Refuge and the Columbia Bottomlands National Wildlife Refuge, along with the Attwater Prairie Chicken National Wildlife Refuge near Sealy in Austin County. Together, these national wildlife refuges account for large conserved acreages; the Brazoria and Anahuac refuges alone total more than 70,000 acres.

Two other classes of federally protected or semi-protected lands are the holdings of the National Park Service and U.S. Forest Service. The Big Thicket National Preserve covers approximately 100,000 acres at the time of writing, consisting primarily of linear holdings along Village Creek and the Neches River. The 163,000 acres of the Sam Houston National Forest are wholly within the Houston Wilderness area, as is a portion of the Angelina National Forest. Some zones of these national forests are set aside as wilderness, or for endangered species or trails, but there is also substantial timber harvesting in other sectors.

The State of Texas is a substantial landowner. The Texas Parks and Wildlife Department has both state parks and wildlife management areas. Three parks notable for wildlife are Sea Rim State Park near Sabine Pass; Galveston Island State Park on the island's west end and Brazos Bend State Park on the Brazos River southwest of Houston. The state's wildlife management areas are open to hunting during the appropriate seasons. These include the J. D. Murphree WMA near Port Arthur, Peach Point WMA near Freeport and Mad Island near Palacios. All three offer excellent duck hunting. Together, the wildlife management areas cover more than 40,000 acres.

The State of Texas also has an easement to keep our beaches open. All beaches fronting the Gulf of Mexico are subject to the Open Beaches Act, which has its origins in Spanish civil law recognizing a public right of access and usage. Similarly, the state owns the bottoms of the bays and the bottom of the Gulf of Mexico out three leagues (approximately ten miles). Management of these lands is placed in the Texas General Land Office, which is governed by an elected commissioner.

Added to these categories are the parks owned and maintained by county and city governments throughout the region. Some of the more important waterways are beginning to be dotted by publicly owned lands within urbanized areas, particularly in Harris and Fort Bend counties, where extensive trail systems are being developed along the Brazos River and Cypress and Spring creeks.

And not to be forgotten in the protection of public lands are the ongoing efforts of nonprofit organizations, which make a huge difference in our ability to buy and set aside important areas. Both statewide and local organizations play significant roles. The Nature Conservancy of Texas, for example, owns and protects three major tracts in the Houston Wilderness area: the Mad Island Preserve near Palacios, the Sandylands Sanctuary in the Big Thicket, and the Texas City Prairie Preserve, where the most resilient population of the critically endangered Attwater's prairie-chicken is found.

Another group purchasing large tracts is the

Conservation Fund, which has been buying and protecting Big Thicket lands recently released for sale by several timber companies, offering a once-in-a-lifetime chance to add to the inventory of natural lands in this important ecoregion. Similarly, the Trust for Public Lands is active in purchasing lands. These groups purchase tracts and then sell them at cost to the U.S. Fish and Wildlife Service when the agency has funds available. Such private groups can move fast to secure the land and then recoup the investment later so as to move forward to the next deal.

Several local nonprofit groups have made a profound difference by buying land and holding it for conservation purposes. The Houston Audubon Society owns two of the most important preserves for birdwatching—the High Island Woods and the Bolivar Flats, both famous with birders from around the world. The society also owns several other tracts in the region.

The Katy Prairie Conservancy is dedicated to protecting the Katy Prairie west of Houston in Harris, Waller and Fort Bend counties. The Katy Prairie is important to wintering waterfowl and also acts as a sponge to hold storm water that otherwise would flow into Houston. Since its formation in 1992, the conservancy has purchased significant acreage, primarily on or near Cypress Creek as it cuts across the prairie. Its long-term goal is to preserve 50,000 to 60,000 acres of the Katy Prairie, or a quarter of its historical extent, through purchases, conservation easements and management agreements. The organization has just recently purchased a majority interest in a 6,478-acre tract of land known as the Warren Ranch. It is one of the last remaining large family farms still participating in agriculture on the Katy Prairie. While functioning as a working farm, albeit an altered prairie system, it provides invaluable habitat for a wide range of species.

The Legacy Land Trust holds conservation easements and manages properties that have been set aside for conservation purposes. In many respects, this is the ultimate free market/private landowner solution to conserving lands without giving up ownership. As of 2006, the trust held conservation easements over nearly 5,000 acres of land in the immediate vicinity of Houston.

Armand Bayou is a beautiful bayou that flows into Clear Lake near NASA's Johnson Space Center. In 1974, the Armand Bayou Nature Center was formed and dedicated to the protection of a heavily wooded tract bordering this bayou and the tidal waters of Galveston Bay. Here, on a 2,500-acre preserve, one finds interpretive trails and guides to help in understanding the floodplain forest and wetlands that once bordered much of Clear Lake.

The Buffalo Bayou Partnership coordinates the integration of major amenities into the Bayou greenbelt and seeks ways to increase community involvement through pedestrian, boating and biking amenities, permanent and temporary art installations and other natural and built attractions. Along with teams of tireless Green Team Volunteers the Partnership has conducted dozens of cleanups and restoration projects to improve habitat quality and biodiversity within the Bayou corridor. In the past seven years, the Partnership has raised and leveraged over $45 million for improvements along a ten-mile stretch of Buffalo Bayou.

Together, the federal, state and local governments have formed a partnership with nongovernmental organizations to protect our natural capital. They have done an excellent job with limited financial resources. As more come to realize and treasure the incredible resources our area is blessed with, we hope these funds will grow and a new generation of environmental stewards will arise to meet the challenges of the future.

# Ecological Services

## Ecological Services and Urbanization

One way to view the resources of timber, water and land that early settlers found here is as "ecological capital," or the irreplaceable endowment of natural assets of an area. When settlers came to exploit the bountiful natural resources through their new livelihoods of logging and ranching, they converted ecological capital into economic capital. In itself, a forest of standing trees had little economic value to settlers, but through the simple act of cutting, the trees came to be worth a great deal of money.

The emergence and growth of cities and their switch from small centers to absolute dominance in population marked a turning point in human and environmental history. This shift reshaped cities themselves as well as rural areas, a larger share of which was converted to serving the needs of urban populations. As the economy and population grew, natural resources became scarcer, depleting much of the original ecological capital of the area. Although cities represent only about one percent of the earth's land surface, their actual ecological footprint is far larger as they draw in food, water, energy and land for growth and waste disposal.

The Houston region's population is expected to exceed 5 million by 2025. The additional land area and water supply that will be required to accommodate this growing population will place heavier demands on our remaining ecological capital without careful planning. Due to changes in workplace culture and affordability of technology, people are able to live even farther from the urban center. With these shifts in work practices, more roads are built in rural areas, leading to more housing and shopping developments, churches and schools at a cost of losing some of our agricultural heritage.

As we grow, we are recognizing that our threat-

*Recreational opportunities are just one benefit of conservation included in the many more valuable ecological services that the ecosystem provides.*

ened landscapes are worthy of our stewardship and protection. Today, urban areas and their associated activities are important components of the ecosystem. We can no longer think of cities and development as separate from the surrounding resources; we can no longer ignore the impact of urbanization on remaining ecological capital. Fortunately, new approaches to urban design are emerging. The challenge for the region now is to adapt these new paradigms of growth to our political, economic and social culture and to adopt conservation strategies that ensure quality of life and preservation of ecological capital. The point about capital, of course, is to use the earned interest but not dent the holdings.

## The Value of Ecological Services

Most of us rarely consider the fundamental life-support services that ecosystems provide and on which human well-being depends. Butterflies are pretty, and bees can be scary, but how often do we recall the key services that bees and butterflies perform by pollinating plants, including the plants bearing the foods we eat?

Trees are decorative and offer welcome shade, but in addition to being a source of lumber they play an even more important role in processing the air we breathe. And they are on duty twenty-four hours a day. Similarly, wetlands are at work all day, every day, naturally purifying the water we drink. If human technology had to perform all these services due to the loss of existing ecosystems, the economic costs to society would be nothing short of staggering.

Ecosystem services are the processes whereby the environment produces resources that we usually take for granted: clean water, timber, and habitat for fisheries, and pollination of native and agricultural plants. Ecosystems provide a wide array of services that perform many essential

*Greenways within cities, where native vegetation can flourish, help protect areas from erosion and provide habitat for wildlife.*

*Tree cover within urban areas abates air pollution and reduces the heat island effect.*

functions, including:

- Moderating weather extremes and their impacts
- Dispersing seeds
- Protecting areas from erosion
- Detoxifying and decomposing wastes
- Controlling pests
- Maintaining biodiversity
- Generating and preserving soils
- Purifying air and water
- Pollinating crops and natural vegetation

Ecosystem services are threatened when consumption, population growth and the impacts of technology are too great for the natural environment to absorb. Many human activities disrupt, impair or reengineer ecosystems to the point where they can no longer perform their critical services. These activities may include deforestation; pollution of land, water and air; overfishing; soil depletion and erosion; introduction of exotic species; use of pesticides and other chemicals; and destruction of wetlands.

Greater Houston's network of bayous, for example, offers a series of local ecosystem services. Bayous in their natural state provide habitat for a wide variety of birds, small mammals, reptiles, fish and other aquatic creatures. Natural bayous also serve as natural flood protection and in addition, the bayous enhance our well-being and quality of life through scenic beauty and opportunities for recreation such as canoeing, walking, running and fishing. Some of our region's bayous such as Armand Bayou, Clear Creek and Cypress Creek, to name a few, are models of well-preserved naturally functioning bayous, demonstrating the need for these ecological assets in our region.

Similarly, the region's extensive tree cover is a major asset worth protecting for all the services it provides, including its role in removal of air pollution. As described in the recent study, Houston's Regional Forest, we need to monitor and guide the development of the area's green infrastructure. Forest cover can be compromised by urban development, but it can also be safeguarded through awareness of the benefits of forest functions and values (see http://www.houstonregionalforest.org/Report/).

The region's leaders are becoming aware that the true value of bayous and forests reaches far beyond aesthetic appeal. A challenge to more effective planning and decision-making regarding the preservation of bayous—or any other natural resource that provides ecological services—is the lack of a precise valuation of these services. Without such explicit economic representation of the value of these resources in providing ecosystem services, it may be difficult for planners and decision-makers to consider ecosystem needs along with the clearly expressed needs of agriculture, industry and municipalities when they compete for resources.

An important new area of endeavor called ecological economics works to derive dollar values for natural resources and the ecosystem services they provide. This emerging science uses sophisticated economic valuation techniques to develop such monetary estimates. Ecological economists anticipate that their estimates of the very substantial value provided by natural resources and ecological services will help planners, developers, elected officials and environmental advocates make choices that lead to more effective stewardship and sustainable use of unique and irreplaceable natural resources.

# Stewardship

*One unique way to get out and experience the Houston Wilderness region is by canoe.*

*The Chinese Tallow tree,* Triadica sebifera, *is one of several invasive species that is threatening the natural ecosystems of the Houston Wilderness region.*

## Stewardship

The most striking aspect of the spectacular natural area we call Houston Wilderness is its great diversity, and the land ownership is as diverse as the habitat. Within our twenty-four counties are large acreages devoted to agriculture and timber production, and wonderful protected areas, but also one of the largest industrial complexes in the world, accompanied by vast urban sprawl. The ownership and management philosophies of the system of protected public lands, parks and preserves are themselves quite varied, thus there are as many different approaches to stewardship as there are conservation goals.

Some of the protected areas have been set aside for conservation of migratory waterfowl and provide for outdoor recreation in the form of birding and hunting. Other areas have been protected for their biological diversity, including units of the Big Thicket National Preserve and holdings of the Nature Conservancy of Texas. Still other jewels of the system have been set aside for education and recreation. Given this kind of diversity, both in the natural systems represented and in the philosophies of the entities with management responsibility, there are overarching issues of stewardship, and there should be some common goals.

Among the significant stewardship challenges we face is the dramatic proliferation of invasive species of flora and fauna. Throughout the coastal prairies, for example, Chinese tallow trees threaten the very existence of the native ecosystem. In freshwater ponds and lakes throughout the region, exotic aquatic plants such as hydrilla and giant salvinia can spread at alarming rates if not checked. One destructive introduced animal that has become widespread is the feral hog. No matter the original purpose of the protected area or the nature of ownership, every effort should be made to remove and erad-

icate such invaders, as they ultimately place at risk the purposes for which these parks and preserves were established in the first place, in addition to compromising their continued viability for preservation and recreation.

Water presents another challenge. All our natural systems are dependent on water in one way or another. Water is the source of all life. In many areas, engineering changes for drainage, navigation, water supply and other purposes has significantly altered the natural flows necessary to maintain terrestrial as well as aquatic ecosystems. Ensuring sufficient water to maintain the biological integrity of these systems will be an issue for both science and public policy and will require constant attention in the years ahead.

Several key principles should guide stewardship of all sites, irrespective of ownership. Areas within the system should not be managed for single species of animals or plants but for the widest possible biological diversity. We must always bear in mind that protecting the land without managing it, or without assuring sufficient water to maintain diversity, will be inadequate to protect its long-term values. Public access for appropriate recreation and environmental education should also be provided.

## Future of Houston Wilderness

The ecological assets of the Houston Wilderness are an immense set of capital holdings that produce ecosystem services, recreational value and scenic beauty. Our ecosystems are among the most significant representations of natural diversity in the United States, and an effort to protect much of the region is under way.

The natural bounty of the region helps make Texas the number one-hunting state in America and the number-two fishing state. In spite of all the impacts to its resources over the years,

Galveston Bay remains the most productive recreational and commercial fishery in Texas. Thanks to the critical marsh and prairie habitats for migratory waterfowl and the irreplaceable bottomland hardwood forests so essential to neotropical birds, the upper Texas coast is one of the top destinations in the world for birders.

All this surrounds an industrial complex that consumes twice as much energy as any other place in the country. All this is in the neighborhood of the nation's fourth-largest city and a major port, in a state where the population is expected to double in the next generation. The growth in human numbers is especially meaningful for greater Houston in that it continues to push the urban complex ever westward and into some of the most distinctive bottomland hardwood forests and coastal prairies in the hemisphere.

These conditions and the anticipated continued economic growth of the region pose both great opportunities and immense challenges. The greatest threat to the rural landscape is the continued fragmentation of family lands. The pressures of estate and property taxes along with encroaching urban development are forcing private landowners to sell, resulting in breakup of habitat into smaller and smaller parcels that are difficult to manage for diversity. This same growth is placing an ever-growing strain on continued supplies of fresh water so necessary for the nourishment of our bays and estuaries and the health of the forests.

As our urban population increases and becomes dramatically more diverse, we must redouble efforts to introduce urban children to the wonders, joys and fun in the natural landscape, and to the role of ecosystems as natural capital, or in time there will be no one to defend it or take care of it for the future.

We must also continue to advocate for additional land conservation funding. The amount of money available for the purchase of wildlife refuges, state parks, conservation easements and local parks is the lowest in a generation, and only pressure from those who love wild places and understand their importance in the larger scheme of things will ensure the restoration of such funding. Because we do not have the same level of federal protection afforded most western states, it is truly up to the private citizens, environmentalists, elected officials and others to continue efforts at conserving our region's natural treasures.

Our leaders and our people of the Houston Wilderness region have the power and vision to make conservation a reality. To protect, preserve and promote the unique biodiversity of the region's precious remaining ecological capital, through a broad-based alliance of business, environmental and government interests, Houston Wilderness acts as a bridge between a dynamic, growing city and the wetlands, forests, prairies and river systems that sustain us as individuals and communities. We recognize that quality of life and wilderness are bound to one another. To ensure we will always have these natural resources, we strive to share the beauty and create awareness of what has been generously loaned to us. We spend our weekends hiking in ancient pine forests, canoeing winding bayous, or watching colorful songbirds on their migration route.

We work for people and communities, and know that we can all prosper and grow through our connection to wilderness. We are educators in search of opportunities to expand knowledge and instill an ethic. We are benefactors and stewards of a rich natural history. We are future generations who will enjoy and benefit from the wilderness as those who came before us did.

We are Houston Wilderness. *It's our nature.*

*Hands-on activities engage children and adults alike at Sea Center Texas, and help visitors understand and appreciate the natural world.*

*Environmental education programs, such as this one at Matagorda Bay Nature Park, help to educate a young generation of environmental stewards.*

# Further Reading

Abernethy, Francis E. (editor). *Tales from the Big Thicket.* Temple Big Thicket Series no. 1. Denton:University of North Texas Press, 2002.

Antrobus, Sally E. *Galveston Bay.* College Station: Texas A&M University Press, 2005.

Aten, Lawrence E. *Indians of the Upper Texas Coast.* New York: Academic Press, 1983.

Blackburn, James B. *The Book of Texas Bays.* Photos by Jim Olive. College Station: Texas A&M University Press, 2004.

Cabeza de Vaca, Alvar Nuñez. *Cabeza de Vaca's Adventures in the Unknown Interior of America.* Translated and edited by C. Covey. Albuquerque: University of New Mexico Press, 1961.

Cartwright, Gary. *Galveston: A History of the Island.* New York: Atheneum-Macmillan, 1991.

Chipman, Donald E. *Spanish Texas 1519–1821.* Austin: University of Texas Press, 1992.

Clay, John V. *Spain, Mexico and the Lower Trinity: An Early History of the Texas Gulf Coast.* Baltimore: Gateway Press, 1987.

Corzine, James J., Jr. *Saving the Big Thicket: From Exploration to Preservation, 1685–2003.* Denton: University of North Texas Press and Big Thicket Association, 2004.

Daniels, A. Pat. *Bolivar! Gulf Coast Peninsula.* Crystal Beach: Peninsula Press of Texas, 1985.

Davis, W. B., and D. J. Schmidly. *The Mammals of Texas.* Austin: Texas Parks and Wildlife Press, 1994.

Donovan, Richard. *Paddling the Wild Neches.* College Station: Texas A&M University Press, 2006.

Dyes, John C. *Nesting Birds of the Coastal Islands: A Naturalist's Year on Galveston Bay.* Austin: University of Texas Press, 1993.

Epperson, Jean L. *Lost Spanish Towns: Atascosito and Trinidad de Salcedo.* Hemphill, Texas: Dogwood Press, 1996.

Eubanks, Ted L. Jr., Robert A. Behrstock, and Ron J. Weeks. *Birdlife of Houston, Galveston, and the Upper Texas Coast.* College Station: Texas A&M University Press, 2006.

Folmer, H. "De Bellisle on the Texas Coast." *Southwestern Historical Quarterly* 44, no. 2 (1940): 204–231.

Foster, William C. *Spanish Expeditions into Texas 1689–1768.* Austin: University of Texas Press, 1995.

Freeman, M. D., and T. H. Hale, Jr. Cypress Creek: *Reconnaissance Survey and Assessment of Prehistoric and Historical Resources, Cypress Creek Watershed in Harris and Waller Counties, Texas.* Research Report no. 68, Texas Archeological Survey. Austin: University of Texas, 1978.

Galveston Bay Estuary Program (GBEP). *State of the Bay: A Characterization of the Galveston Bay Ecosystem.* 2nd ed. Houston: GBEP and Environmental Institute of Houston, University of Houston–Clear Lake, 2002.

Gilmore, Kathleen. "French, Spanish, and Indian Interaction in Colonial Texas." *Bulletin of the Texas Archeological Society* 63 (1992): 123–133.

*Great Texas Coastal Birding Trail: Upper Texas Coast* (map, www.tpwd.state.tx.us/huntwild/wild/wildlife_trails/coastal/). Austin: Texas Parks and Wildlife Department, 2001.

Gulf Restoration Network. *Destruction by Design: Army Corps of Engineers' Continuing Assault on America's Environment.* Comp. Mark Beorkrem and Cynthia Sarthou; ed. Heidi Lovett. New Orleans: GRN, 1999.

Gunter, Pete. *The Big Thicket: A Challenge for Conservation.* New York: Viking Press, 1971.

Gunter, Pete A. Y. *The Big Thicket: An Ecological Reevaluation.* Denton: University of North Texas Press, 1993.

Henson, Margaret, and Kevin Ladd. *Chambers County: A Pictorial History.* Norfolk, Va.: Donning Company, 1988.

*The Historic Seacoast of Texas.* Paintings by J. U. Salvant. Essays by David G. McComb. Austin: University of Texas Press, 1999.

*Houston's Regional Forest: Structure, Functions, and Values.* Houston: U.S. Forest Service, Texas Forest Service, and Houston Advanced Research Center, 2005.

Kavanagh, James. *Houston Birds: An Introduction to Familiar Species of the Upper Texas Coast.* Pocket Naturalist guide. Phoenix: Waterford Press, 2001.

Larson, Erik. *Isaac's Storm: A Man, a Time, and the Deadliest Hurricane in History.* New York: Crown Publishers, 1999.

Loughmiller, Campbell and Lynn (compilers and editors). *Big Thicket Legacy.* Foreword by Francis E. Abernethy. Temple Big Thicket Series no. 2. Denton: University of North Texas Press, 2002.

McComb, David G. *Galveston: A History.* Austin: University Of Texas Press, 1986.

Mitchell, Forrest L., and James L. Lasswell. *A Dazzle of Dragonflies.* College Station: Texas A&M University Press, 2006.

Moore, Roger G., and Madeleine J. Donachie. "The Southeast Texas Indian Response to European Incursion." *Bulletin of the Texas Archeological Society* 72 (2001): 55–61.

Moore, Francis, Jr.  Map and Description of Texas: Containing Sketches of its History, Geology, Geography and Statistics.  Waco: Texian Press, 1965.

Moulton, Daniel W., and John S. Jacob. *Texas Coastal Wetlands Guidebook.* Texas Sea Grant Publication TAMU-SG-00-605. Bryan: Sea Grant, 2000.

National Wildlife Federation. *Higher Ground: A Report on Voluntary Property Buyouts in the Nation's Floodplains.* Washington, D.C.: National Wildlife Federation, 1998.

Olmsted, Frederick Law. *A Journey through Texas* [1857]. Reprint, Austin: Von Boeckmann-Jones Press, 1962.

Patterson, Leland W. "The Archeology of Inland Southeast Texas: A Quantitative Study." *Bulletin of the Texas Archeological Society* 61 (1990): 255–280.

Perttula, Timothy K. "The Great Kingdom of the Tejas: The Life and Times of Caddo Peoples in Texas between ca. 1530–1859." *Bulletin of the Texas Archeological Society* 72 (2001): 73–89.

Robison, B. C. *Birds of Houston.* Photos by John L. Tveten. Austin: University of Texas Press, 1996.

Sansom, A. *Texas Lost: Vanishing Heritage.* Photos by Wyman Meinzer. Dallas: Parks and Wildlife Foundation of Texas, 1996.

Schmidly, David J. *Texas Natural History: A Century of Change.* Lubbock: Texas Tech University Press, 2002.

Sullivan, Jerry. *An Atlas of Biodiversity: Chicago Wilderness, a Regional Nature Reserve.* Chicago: Chicago Region Biodiversity Council, 1997.

*Texas Beach and Bay Access Guide.* Austin: Texas General Land Office, 2002.

Tveten, John L. *Exploring the Bayous.* New York: David McKay Company, 1979.

Tveten, John, and Gloria Tveten. *Butterflies of Houston and Southeast Texas.* Austin: University of Texas Press, 1996.

Watson, Geraldine Ellis. *Big Thicket Plant Ecology: An Introduction.* 3rd edition. College Station: Texas A&M University Press, 2006.

Weddle, Robert S. "Spanish Exploration of the Texas Coast, 1519–1800." *Bulletin of the Texas Archeological Society* 63 (1992): 99–122.

Winningham, Geoff. *Along Forgotten River.* Austin: Texas State Historical Association, 2003.

# Houston Wilderness
## and partner organizations

### Houston Wilderness

Houston Wilderness is a broad-based alliance of business, environmental and government interests that act in concert to protect, preserve and promote the unique biodiversity of the region's precious remaining ecological capital while recognizing the importance of the region's natural assets to its cultural history, economic vitality and future well-being.

### Houston Wilderness Officers

Brad Raffle, Chairman of the Board
Rosie Zamora, President
Jim Blackburn, Vice President
Jim Kollaer, Vice President
Diane Schenke, Secretary-Treasurer

### Houston Wilderness Executive Council

Joel Bartsch, Houston Museum of Natural Science
Jim Blackburn, Blackburn & Carter
Todd Brindle, Big Thicket National Preserve
Robert C. Brown, III, Greater Ft. Bend County Economic
    Development Council
Kirstin Cannon, PricewaterhouseCoopers, L.L.P.
Shawn Gross, SAJG Investments, Inc.
Charlie Herder, Colliers International
Jerry Hopkins, Texas Parks & Wildlife
Bill Jones, Vinson & Elkins, L.L.P.
Andy Jones, The Conservation Fund
Jim Kollaer, The Staubach Company
Ann Lents, Center for Houston's Future
Jennifer Lorenz, Legacy Land Trust
Oniel Mendenhall, Trini & O.C. Mendenhall Foundation
Joy Nicholopoulos, U.S. Fish & Wildlife
Carter Perrin, Perrin Interests
Brad Raffle, Conservation Capital
Beth Robertson, Westview Development, Inc.
Diane Schenke, The Park People
Robert J. Stokes, Jr., Galveston Bay Foundation
Margaret Vaughan-Robinson, MVC Consulting
Rosie Zamora, Houston Wilderness

### Houston Wilderness Staff

Rosie Zamora, President
Victoria Herrin, Trails Coordinator
Kim Matlock, Accountant
Lauren Minarcik, Project Coordinator
Trey Nall, Website Coordinator
Holly Thorson, Assistant to the President

### Organizations of the Houston Wilderness Network

The organization currently has fifty-five partner organizations in its Houston Wilderness Network. All network members share a commitment to cooperate and work together to further the mission of Houston Wilderness. The member organizations of the Houston Wilderness Network, and the thousands of volunteers who work with them, are pooling their resources and expertise to most effectively protect, preserve and promote the natural heritage of the southeast Texas region.

### Network Members

**Armand Bayou Nature Center, Inc.**
Post Office Box 58828
Houston, Texas 77258
281-474-2551
www.abnc.org

**Bayou Preservation Association, Inc.**
3201 Allen Parkway, Suite 200
Houston, Texas 77019
713-529-6443
www.bayoupreservation.org

**Baytown Nature Center**
201 1/2 West Schreck
Baytown, Texas 77520
281-420-5360
www.baytownnaturecenter.org

**Big Thicket Association**
Post Office Box 198
Saratoga, Texas 77585
936-262-8522
www.btatx.org/

**Big Thicket National Preserve**
3785 Milam
Beaumont, Texas 77701
409-839-2689
www.nps.gov/bith

**Brazos Bend State Park**
21901 F.M. 762
Needville, Texas 77461
979-553-5101
www.tpwd.state.tx.us/park/brazos

**Brazos Bend State Park Volunteer Organization**
21901 F.M. 762
Needville, Texas 77461
979-553-5101
www.bbspvo.org

**Brazos Valley Museum of Natural History**
3232 Briarcrest Drive
Bryan, Texas 77802
979-776-2195
http://bvmuseum.myriad.net

**Buffalo Bayou Partnership**
1113 Vine Street, Suite 200
Houston, Texas 77002
(713) 752-0314
www.buffalobayou.org

**Christmas Bay Foundation**
4709 Austin Street
Houston, Texas 77004
(713) 524-1012
www.christmasbay.org

**Colorado River Foundation**
P.O. Box 50029
Austin, Texas 78763-0029
512-458-8844
www.coloradoriver.org

**Cypress Creek Flood Control Coalition**
12526 Texas Army Trail
Cypress, Texas 77429
281-469-5161
www.ccfcc.org

**Eddie V. Gray Wetlands Education and Recreation Center**
1724 Market Street
Baytown, Texas 77520
281-420-7101
http://tourismprod.baytown.org/Wetlands+Center/

**Galveston Bay Conservation & Preservation Association**
Post Office Box 323
Seabrook, Texas 77586
281-326-3343
www.gbcpa.net

**Galveston Bay Estuary Program**
17041 El Camino Real, Suite 210
Houston, Texas 77058
(281) 218-6461
www.gbep.state.tx.us

**Galveston Bay Foundation**
17324-A Highway 3
Webster, Texas 77598
281-332-3381
www.galvbay.org

**Galveston Bay Watershed Academic Partnership YouthLaunch**
17324-A Highway 3
Webster, TX 77598
281-332-3381 ext 213 (Houston)
800-875-1862 (Austin)
www.earthforce.org/section/offices/texas/gbwap/

**Galveston Island Nature Tourism Council Inc.**
Post Office Box 1468
Galveston, Texas 77553-1468
409-392-0841
www.galvestonfeatherfest.com

**George Ranch Historical Park**
10215 FM 762
Richmond, Texas 77469
281-343-0218
www.georgeranch.org

**Greater Houston Partnership**
1200 Smith, Suite 700
Houston, Texas 77002
713-844-3600
www.houston.org

**Gulf Coast Bird Observatory**
103 West Highway 332
Lake Jackson, Texas 77566
979-480-0999
www.gcbo.org

**Gulf Coast Institute**
3015 Richmond, Suite 250
Houston, Texas 77098
713-523-5757
www.gulfcoastideas.org

# (Network Organizations continued)

**Hermann Park Conservancy**
6201 A Golf Course Drive
Houston, Texas 77030
(713) 524-5876
www.hermannpark.org

**Houston Advanced Research Center**
4800 Research Forest Drive, Building 2
The Woodlands, Texas 77381
281-367-1348
www.harc.edu

**Houston Arboretum and Nature Center**
4501 Woodway Drive
Houston, Texas 77024
713-681-8433
www.houstonarboretum.org

**Houston Archeological Society**
P.O. Box 6751
Houston, Texas 77265-6751
www.houstonarcheology.org

**Houston Audubon Society**
440 Wilchester Boulevard
Houston, Texas 77079
713-932-1639
www.houstonaudubon.org

**Houston-Galveston Area Council**
Post Office Box 22777
Houston, Texas 77227-2777
713-627-3200
www.h-gac.com

**Houston Museum of Natural Science**
One Hermann Circle Drive
Houston, Texas 77030
(713) 639-4629
www.hmns.org

**Houston Parks Board**
2001 Kirby Drive, Suite 814
Houston, Texas 77019
(713) 942-8500
www.houstonparksboard.org

**Houston Zoo, Inc.**
1513 N. MacGregor
Houston, Texas 77030
713-533-6500
www.houstonzoo.org

**Jesse H. Jones Park and Nature Center**
20634 Kenswick Drive
Humble, Texas 77338
281-446-8588
www.cp4.hctx.net/jones

**Katy Prairie Conservancy**
3015 Richmond Avenue, Suite 230
Houston, Texas 77098-3114
713-523-6135
www.katyprairie.org

**Kids' Environmental Education Project (K.E.E.P.)**
Post Office Box 440490
Houston, Texas 77244-0490
281-759-8343
www.cechouston.org/CEC/?p=41

**Legacy Land Trust**
Post Office Box 980816
Houston, Texas 77098-0816
713-524-2100
www.llt.org

**Matagorda County Birding Nature Center**
P.O. Box 2212
Bay City, Texas 77414
979-245-3336
www.mcbnc.org

**Nature Discovery Center**
7112 Newcastle
Bellaire, Texas 77401
713-667-6550
www.naturediscoverycenter.org

**National Wildlife Federation**
Gulf States Natural Resource Center
44 East Avenue Suite 200
Austin, Texas 78701
512-610-7768
www.nwf.org

**Rice University**
6100 Main Street
Houston, Texas 77005
713-348-0000
www.rice.edu

**Scenic Galveston**
20 Colony Park Circle
Galveston, Texas 77551
409-744-7431
www.scenicgalveston.org

**Student Conservation Association**
1800 North Kent Street, Suite 102
Arlington, Virginia 22209
703-524-2441
www.thesca.org

**Scenic Houston**
3015 Richmond Avenue, Suite 220
Houston, Texas 77098
713-629-0481
www.scenichouston.org

**Texas Forest Service**
301 Tarrow Drive, Suite 364
College Station, Texas 77840-7896
979-458-6600
http://txforestservice.tamu.edu

**Texas Parks & Wildlife Department, Region 4**
105 San Jacinto
La Porte, Texas 77571
281-471-3200
www.tpwd.state.tx.us

**Texas R.I.C.E.**
1204 Hodges Lane
Wharton, Texas 77488
979-578-0100
www.karankawa.com/rice.htm

**The Children's Museum of Houston**
1500 Binz
Houston, Texas 77004
713-522-5747
www.cmhouston.org

**The Conservation Fund, Texas Office**
101 West Sixth Street, Suite 601
Austin, Texas 78701
512-477-1712
www.conservationfund.org

**The Memorial Park Conservancy, Inc.**
P.O. Box 131024
Houston , TX 77219
voice (713) 863-8403
fax (713) 863-9348
www.memorialparkconservancy.org

**The Nature Conservancy of Texas**
4702 Highway 146 North
Texas City, Texas 77590
409-941-9114
www.tnc.org

**The Park People**
3015 Richmond Avenue, Suite 210
Houston, Texas 77098
713-942-7275
www.parkpeople.org

**The Quality of Life Coalition**
1200 Smith, Suite 700
Houston, Texas 77002
713-844-3627
www.qolhouston.org

**The Trust for Public Land**
1113 Vine Street, Suite 200
Houston, Texas 77002
713-226-7200
www.tpl.org

**Trees for Houston**
3100 Weslayan, Suite 305
Houston, Texas 77027
713-840-8733
www.treesforhouston.org

**Upper Texas Coast Waterborne Education Center**
207 Miller Street
Post Office Box 9
Anahuac, Texas 77514
409-267-3547
www.txwaterborne.org

**Urban Harvest**
Post Office Box 980460
Houston, Texas 77098
713-880-5540
www.urbanharvest.org

**Wallisville Lake Project**
20020 IH 10 East Feeder Road
Wallisville, Texas 77597
409-389-2285
www.swg.usace.army.mil/items/Wallisville/

# Acknowledgments

### Acknowledgements

Many people contributed to this Atlas by providing information, advice and review of manuscripts. The list includes:

Mark Kramer and George Regmund of the Armand Bayou Nature Center; Kevin Shanley and Mary Ellen Whitworth of the Bayou Preservation Association; Debra Shore of Chicago Wilderness; Andy Dearwater, Danny Rigg and James Petty of Dearwater Design; Roland Adamson of George Ranch Historical Park; Cecilia Riley and John Arvin of the Gulf Coast Bird Observatory; Hayden Haucke of the Gus Engleling Wildlife Management Area; Winnie Burkett, Flo Hannah and Joy Hester of the Houston Audubon Society; Mike Howlett of Jesse H. Jones Park and Nature Center; Mary Anne Piacentini of the Katy Prairie Conservancy; Stephanie Glenn, Will Alvis, Todd Mitchell, Marilu Hastings and Jim Lester of the Houston Advanced Research Center; Diane Schenke of The Park People; Ross Carrie of Raven Environmental Services; Brandt Mannchen of the Sierra Club; Larry Brown of the Spring Branch Science Center; Peter Conaty of St. Mary's Episcopal Church, West Columbia; Monique Reed of Texas A&M University; John Jacob of the Texas Coastal Watershed Program; Terri Ling of Texas Cooperative Extension; Justice Jones of the Texas Forest Service; Bill Balboa, Mike Quinn, Mike Rezsutek and Jim Sutherlin of the Texas Parks & Wildlife Department; Glenn Aumann of the University of Houston Coastal Center; Mike Lange, Stuart Marcus, David Rosen, Terry Rossignol and Jennifer Sanchez of the U.S. Fish & Wildlife Service; Don Greene of Whitewater Experience; Sally Antrobus; Jim Blackburn; Nancy Brown; Gabrielle Cosgriff; Bill Dawson; James B. Ewbank; Will Fleming; Richard D. Jaffe; Jim Kollaer; Ann Lents; David Lewis; Jessica Milne; Jim Neville; Glenn Olsen; Bob Ross; Joe Smith; Sharron Stewart; the Student Conservation Association; Charles Tapley; Don Verser; David Williams.

## Credits

### Chapter Credits

Landscape on the Move, H.C. Clark
Ecoregion Overview, Jim Blackburn
The Wonder of Migration, Michael Berryhill
The Big Thicket, Chuck Hunt
Pineywoods, Michael Berryhill
Trinity Bottomlands, Chuck Hunt
Columbia Bottomlands, Michael Berryhill
Coastal Prairies, Michael Berryhill
Katy Prairie Sidebar, Jim Blackburn & Lauren Minarcik
Post Oak Savannah, Michael Berryhill
Bays & Estuaries, Jim Blackburn
Coastal Marshes, Jim Blackburn
The Gulf of Mexico and Barrier Islands, Jim Blackburn
Bayou Wilderness, Jim Blackburn
Protected Lands, Jim Blackburn
People on the Land, Alecia Gallaway
Ecological Services, Marilu Hastings
Stewardship, Andy Sansom

### Map Credits

The map of Ecological Capital on Page 1 was created by Jim Blackburn and Charles Tapley. All chapter title page maps were created by Houston Advanced Research Center and Dearwater Design. All other maps were created by Dearwater Design.

### Map Sources

All chapter title page maps except People on the Land and Migration, Houston Advanced Research Center and Houston Wilderness. People on the Land chapter title page map, www.lib.utexas.edu/maps/historical/history_texas.html. Migration chapter title page map, Gulf Coast Bird Observatory. Page 4, Geology map, Geological Highway Map of Texas from the American Association of Petroleum Geologists; Page 21, Gulf of Mexico Shoreline Location Changes and p. 94, Bayou Floodplain, Roadside Geology of Texas by Darwin Spearing.

## Photo and Art Credits

Front cover, owl; p. 12, birdwatcher; p. 13, blue grosbeak; p. 19, bobcat; p. 26, Tiger swallowtail, hikers; p. 32, red-cockaded woodpecker; p. 34, otter; p. 38, prothonotary warbler; p. 51, prairie; p. 58, Attwater's Prairie Chicken; p. 60, scissor-tailed flycatcher; p. 66, northern bobwite quail; p. 76, fly-fishing; p. 84, Kemp's Ridley sea turtle; p. 101, dunes; p. 102, Attwater's Prairie Chicken: **Kathy Adams Clark**. Page 68, brown pelican; p. 77, marsh; p. 85, Great egret; pps. 91-92, top, bayou; p. 93, Golden-winged skimmer: **Steve Schuenke**. Pages 1-2, top, biker on path; p. 104, runner on path: **Tom Fox**. Pages 5-6, top, herding cattle; p. 8, cutting sugarcane: **George Ranch Historical Park**. Page 6, hand-drawn illustration of Cabeza de Vaca; p. 29, hand-drawn illustration of fire disturbance; p. 47, hand-drawn illustration of tree leaves; p. 53, hand-drawn illustration of prairie grass root systems; p. 65, hand-drawn illustration of wildflower species: **Andy Dearwater**. Page 6, buffalo: www.photos.com. Page 9, group of men; p. 10, Spindletop oil field, Lucas Gusher: **The Texas Energy Museum**. Page 8, Jean Lafitte; p. 9, Stephen F. Austin: **The Rosenberg Library**. Page 9, plantation kitchen: **Varner Hogg Plantation State Historic Site**. Page 10, slave shackles: **Levi Jordan Plantation Historical Society**. Page IV, least terns, p. 12, snow goose, p. 14, swallow-tailed kite; p. 43, ruby-throated hummingbird; p. 48, black-bellied whistling duck; p. 50, loggerhead shrike, sandhill cranes; p. 51, armadillo; p. 55, raccoon; p. 71, Wilson's plover; p. 74, black skimmer; p. 76, least bittern; p. 80, cottonmouth snake; p. 82, white pelicans; p. 84, American avocet; p. 85, common nighthawk, bottlenose dolphin; p. 90, least terns; p. 95, wood duck; p. 98, green heron; p. 100, northern shoveler: **Mark Bartosik**. Page 13, black witch moth: **Mary M. McGee**. Page 14, monarch butterfly; p. 30, Carolina wren; p. 37, blue heron; p. 38, gray squirrel; p. 46, cedar waxwing, bard owl; p. 55, burrowing owl; p. 56, snow geese; p. 63, bluebonnets; p. 64, coreopsis, p. 68, black-crowned night heron; p. 71, black-necked stilt; p. 72, laughing gulls and Forster's terns; p. 74, red-winged blackbird; p. 77, black-crowned night heron, water lilies, purple gallinule; p. 79, long-billed dowitcher; p. 80, cattle egret; p. 93, hooded warbler: **Wayne Wendel**. Pages 11-12, top, sunset; p. 37, alligator; p. 42, yellow-crowned night heron; p. 43, golden orb spider, alligator, pond sunset; p. 48, bull frog; p. 60, winecups and star daisies; p. 74, Great egret; pps. 105-106, top, bikers on path: **Joe Smith**. Pages 15-16, top, forest floor; p. 19, deer, forest scene; p. 21, Texas trumpets; p. 23, cypress-tupelo swamp; p. 24, flowering dogweed tree; pps. 25-26, top, forest scene; p. 27 winding forest road; p. 29, gulf fritillary, Great egrets; pps. 33-34, top, swamp scene: **Jay Brittain of Temple Inland**. Pages 17-18, top, trees; p. 34, canoeists; p. 35, bald cypress trees; p. 38, Trinity River emptying into bay; p. 66, scissor-tailed flycatcher, red-tailed hawk; p. 98, Buffalo Bayou and downtown Houston; p. 105, canoeists: **Jim Olive**. Page 18, southern blue flag iris; p. 103, father and daughter fishing; p. 104, sunset through the trees: **The Woodlands Operating Company**. Page 18, Lone Star Hiking Trail; pps. 59-60, top, post oak savannah; p. 103, lake: **Tom Flaherty**. Page 19, false turkey tail fungi, p. 24, ringless honey mushroom; p. 35, red-winged blackbird chicks; p. 40, roseate spoonbill family; p. 64, Indian paintbrush; pps. 75-76, top, coastal marsh: **Downs Matthews**. Page 22, colony of Texas trumpets; **Seth Davidson**. Page 30, tickseed; p. 45, golden orb weaver; p. 63, blanket flowers; p. 66, wildflowers along fence; p. 69, lone fisherman on beach; p. 96, orchard orbweaver: **David Williams**. Page 35, alligator; p. 45, black-bellied whistling duck; p. 48, swamp rabbit, red-eared slider turtle: **Phillipe Henry**. Page 35, yellow-crowned night heron: **US Army Corps of Engineers**, Wallisville Lake Project. Pages 41-42, top, tree foliage; p. 61, deer; pps. 83-84, top, birds on beach; p. 92, Great blue heron, fishermen on bayou; p. 93, immature long-horned grasshopper; p. 95, Great blue heron; p. 96, monarch butterfly; p. 98, Great egrets, osprey: **Cliff Meinhardt**. Page 42, radar image: **Sidney Gauthreaux**, Clemson University. Pages 49-50, top, prairie grass; p. 51, immature assassin bug; p. 53, spiderlily, iris; p. 54, water lotus, sensitive briar; p. 58, short-horned grasshopper, black & yellow argiope; pps. 67-68, marsh sunset; p. 82, seaside dragonlet, bull frog, Rambur's forktail; p. 85, evening primrose on beach dunes: **Dennis McKelroy**. Page 79, iris: **Jarrett "Woody" Woodrow**. Page 88, queen parrotfish, jack-knife fish, Atlantic deer cowrie, fire coral with orange sponge and brown chromis: **Frank and Joyce Burek**. Page 87, celebration in Downtown Buffalo Bayou park: **Jim Caldwell**. Pages 99-100, top, Matagorda sunset; p. 106, classroom on the beach: Lower Colorado River Authority, Matagorda Bay Nature Park. Page 102, armadillo: **Martin Dies, Jr. State Park**. Page 105, Chinese tallow tree: **Stephanie Glenn**. Page 106, visitors at touch pool: **Sea Center Texas**.

# Species List

Common Name, *Scientific Name* Page

Acadian flycatcher, *Empidonax virescens* 46

Alligator, *Alligator mississippiensis* 2, 35, 36, 37, 38, 43, 45, 78, 80, 81

Alligator gar, *Atractosteus spatula* 96

American Avocet, *Recurvirostra americana* 84, 86

American beautyberry, *Callicarpa Americana* 22, 64, 95

American beech, *Fagus grandifolia* 20, 22, 23, 30, 44, 47

American Goldfinch, *Carduelis tristis* 37

American holly, *Ilex opaca* 22, 23

American hornbeam, *Carpinus caroliniana* 23

American Kestrel, *Falco sparverius* 54

American Oystercatcher, *Haematopus palliatus* 73

American White Pelican, *Pelecanus erythrorhynchos* 73, 82, 86

American Widgeon duck, *Anas Americana* 80

Anhinga, *Anhinga anhinga* 38

Anna's hummingbird, *Calypte anna* 14

Armadillo, nine-banded, *Dasypus novemcinctus* 51, 96, 102

Arrow-wood viburnum, *Viburnum dentatum* 23

Arctic peregrine falcon, *Falco peregrinus tundrius* 37

Atlantic croaker, *Micropogonias undulatus* 70,87

Atlantic deer cowrie, *Cypraea cervus* 88

Attwater's prairie-chicken, *Tympanuchus cupido attwateri* 50, 57, 58, 101, 102

Bachman's sparrow, *Aimophila aestivalis* 31

Bald cypress, *Taxodium distichum* 8, 20, 23, 35, 36, 37

Bald eagle, *Haliaeetus leucocephalus* 28, 37, 46

Barred owl, *Strix varia* 46

Basket oak (syn. Swamp chestnut oak), *Quercus michauxii* 23

Beaver, *Castor canadensis* 36

Belted Kingfisher, *Megaceryle alcyon* 45, 95

Bermuda grass, *Cynodon dactylon* 64

Big Bluestem, *Andropogon gerardii* 50, 51, 53, 55

Black & Yellow Argiope, *Argiope aurantia* 45, 58

Black bear, Louisiana, *Ursus americanus luteolus* 24, 46, 8

Black gum, *Nyssa sylvatica* 20, 22, 23

Black hickory, *Carya texana* 63

Black skimmer, *Rynchops niger* 74

Black willow, *Salix nigra* 40, 45

Black witch moth, *Erebus odora* 13, 14

Black-bellied whistling duck, *Dendrocygna autumnalis* 45, 48

Blackberry, *Rubus fruticosus* 31

Black-chinned hummingbird, *Archilochus alexandri* 14

Black-crowned Night-Heron, *Nycticorax nycticorax* 68, 73, 77

Blackjack oak, *Quercus marilandica* 22, 63

Black-necked stilt, *Himantopus mexicanus* 71

Blackrush (syn. needlegrass rush), *Juncus roemerianus* 80

Black-tailed jackrabbit, *Lepus californicus* 54

Blue crab, *Callinectes sapidus* 52, 71

Blue grosbeak, *Guiraca caerulea* 13

Blue Jay, *Cyanocitta cristata* 96

Bluebird, *Sialia spp.* 37

Bluejack oak, *Quercus incana* 22

Blue-winged Teal, *Anas discors* 45, 81

Bobcat, *Lynx rufus* 19, 36, 38, 57, 64, 81

Bottlenose dolphin, *Tursiops truncatus* 85, 87

Boxelder maple, *Acer negundo* 45

Brazoria palm, a hybrid of *Sabal mexicana* and *Sabal minor* believed to be a new species 44

Broadwing hawk, *Buteo platypterus* 13

Brown Chromis, *Chromis multilineata* 88

Brown Pelican, *Pelecanus occidentalis* 37, 68, 73, 89

Brown shrimp, *Farfantepenaeus aztecus* 71, 73, 87

Browneyed susans, *Rudbeckia triloba* 64

Brown-headed nuthatch, *Sitta pusilla* 31

Buffalo, *Bison bison* 6, 8, 50

Buff-bellied hummingbird, *Amazilia yucatanensis* 14

Bufflehead, *Bucephala albeola* 73

Bull frog, *Rana catesbeiana* 48, 82

Bumble bee, *Bombus pennsylvanicus* 96

Burrowing owl, *Athene cunicularia* 55

Bushy Bluestem, *Andropogon glomeratus* 52

Buttercup, yellow, Genus: Ranunculus 62, 65

Buttonbush, *Cephalanthus occidentalis* 23

Cacti, Family: *Cactaceae* 20

Camphor daisy, *Rayjacksonia phyllocephala* 65

Canebrake / timber rattlesnake, *Crotalus horridus* 46

Carolina ash, *Fraxinus caroliniana* 23

Carolina jessamine, *Gelsemium sempervirens* 30

Carolina laurelcherry, *Prunus caroliniana* 46

Carolina wren, *Thryothorus ludovicianus* 30, 45

Catfishes, Order: *Siluriformes* 38

Cattle egret, *Bubulcus ibis* 64, 80

Cedar elm, *Ulmus crassifolia* 45

Cedar waxwing, *Bombycilla cedrorum* 46

Cherry laurel, *Prunus laurocerasus* 44, 47

Cherrybark oak, *Quercus pagoda* 23

Chickadees, *Parus spp.* 96

Chinese privet, *Ligustrum sinense* 31

Chinese tallow tree, *Sapium sebiferum* 39, 45, 55, 56, 57, 105

Christmas fern, *Polystichum acrostichoides* 23

Cinnamon fern, *Osmunda cinnamomea* 23

Clapper Rail, *Rallus longirostris* 81

Coastal live oak, *Quercus agrifolia* 13

Common Merganser, *Mergus merganser* 73

Common nighthawk, *Chordeiles minor* 85

Coots, Family: *Rallidae* 81

Cordgrass, *Spartina spp.* 52

Coreopsis, *Coreopsis spp.* 60, 65

Cormorants, *Phalacrocorax spp.* 37, 73

Cottonmouth water moccasin, *Agkistrodon piscivorus* 38, 80

Cottonwood, *Populus deltoides* 45

Coyote, *Canis latrans* 38, 54, 81

Crappies, *Pomoxis spp.* 38

Crested caracara, *Caracara cheriway* 54

Deep-rooted sedge, *Cyperus entrerianus* 57

Dewberry, *Rubus enslenii* 31, 50, 64

Diamondback water snake, *Nerodia rhombifer* 96

Dowitcher, *Limnodromus spp.* 86

Downy woodpecker, *Picoides pubescens* 45

Dwarf sperm whale, *Kogia sima* 87

Eastern Gamagrass, *Tripsacum dactyloides* 50, 51, 55

Evening primrose, Genus: *Oenothera* 85

False Turkey Tail, *Stereum ostrea* 19

Farkleberry, *Vaccinium arboreum* 64

Feral hog, *Sus scrofa* 105

Ferruginous hawk, *Buteo regalis* 54

Fiddler crab, Family: *Ocypodidae* 78

Fire ants, red imported, *Solenopsis invicta* 2, 57, 64

Fire coral, branching or encrusting, *Millepora alcicornis* 88

Flowering Dogwood, *Cornus florida* 22, 24, 31

Forster's terns, *Sterna forsteri* 72

Gadwall, *Anas strepera* 80

Giant cane / Native bamboo, *Arundinaria gigantea* 46

Giant salvinia, *Salvinia molesta* 39, 105

Godwits, *Limosa Brisson* 12

Golden orb web spider, *Nephila clavipes* 43

Goldenrod, *Solidago spp.* 50

Golden-winged skimmer, *Libellula auripennis* 93

Grasshopper sparrow, *Ammodramus savannarum* 52

Gray fox, *Urocyon cinereoargenteus* 36

Gray squirrel, *Sciurus carolinensis* 38, 63

## (Species List continued)

Sperm whales, *Physeter macrocephalus* 87

Spicebush swallowtail, *Papilio (Pterourus) troilus* 58

Spider lily, *Hymenocallis liriosme* 53, 56, 62, 65

Spotted sea trout, *Cynoscion nebulosus* 70, 87

Striped mullet, *Mugil cephalus* 70, 73, 78, 86

Sugar hackberry (syn. sugarberry), *Celtis laevigata* 42, 45, 47

Summer tanager, *Piranga rubra* 20, 37

Swainson's hawk, *Buteo swainsoni* 13

Swainson's warbler, *Limnothlypis swainsonii* 46

Swallow-tailed kite, *Elanoides forficatus* 14, 37

Swamp rabbit, *Sylvilagus aquaticus* 48

Sweetbay, *Laurus nobilis* 20, 22, 23

Sweetgum, *Liquidambar styraciflua* 22, 23

Switchcane, *Arundinaria gigantea ssp. tecta* 30, 31, 46

Switchgrass, *Panicum virgatum* 50, 51, 53, 55

Sycamore, *Platanus occidentalis* 45

Tarpon, *Megalops atlanticus* 87

Texas Aster, *Symphyotrichum eulae* 50

Texas Bluebonnet, *Lupinus texensis* 60, 62, 63, 65, 66

Texas evening-primrose, *Oenothera texensis* 62, 65

Texas Indian paintbrush, *Castilleja foliolosa* 62, 64, 65, 66

Texas ironweed, *Vernonia texana* 23

Texas lantana (syn. Western lantana), *Lantana urticoides (L. horrida)* 65

Texas mulberry, *Morus microphylla* 8

Texas persimmon, *Diospyros texana* 31

Texas poppy-mallow, *Callirhoe scabriuscula* 60, 65

Texas prairie crayfish, *Fallicambarus devastator* 96

Texas prairie dawn flower, *Hymenoxys texana* 53

Texas red oak, *Quercus texana* 22

Texas Tridens, *Tridens texanus* 55

Texas Yellow Star, *Lindheimera texana* 60

Tickseed, *Coreopsis lanceolata* 30

Tiger swallowtail, *Papilio glaucus* 26

Titi, *Cyrilla spp.* 20, 22, 23

Tricolored Heron, *Egretta tricolor* 73

Vermilion Flycatcher, *Pyrocephalus rubinus* 37

Water elm, *Planera aquatica* 23

Water hickory, *Carya aquatica* 23

Water lilies, *Nymphaea odorata* 77

Water lotus, *Nelumbo lutea* 54

Water oak, *Quercus nigra* 23, 45

Wax myrtle, *Morella cerifera* 22, 31

Western grebe, *Aechmophorus occidentalis* 80

Western soapberry, *Sapindus saponaria* 45

White ibis, *Eudocimus albus* 45, 78

White oak, *Quercus alba* 22, 23, 36

White prickly poppy, *Argemone polyanthemos* 62

White shrimp, *Litopenaus setiferus* 78, 87

White-tailed deer, *Odocoileus virginianus* 8, 19, 36, 38, 51, 54, 61, 63

Whooping crane, *Grus americana* 52, 57

Wigeongrass, *Ruppia maritima* 80

Wild celery, *Apium graveolens* 80

Wild plum (syn. Peachbush), *Prunus texana* 31

Wild turkey, *Meleagris gallopavo* 46, 63, 64

Willow oak, *Quercus phellos* 23

Wilson's plover, *Charadrius wilsonia* 71

Winged elm, *Ulmus alata* 63

Wood duck, *Aix sponsa* 45, 95, 96

Wood stork, *Mycteria americana* 37

Yaupon, *Ilex vomitoria* 22, 23, 64, 95

Yellow Rail, *Coturnicops noveboracensis* 81

Yellow Trumpet (syn. Texas Trumpet), *Sarracenia alata* 21, 22

Yellow-crowned night heron, *Nyctanassa violacea* 35, 42

Yucca, *Yucca glauca* 20, 22

# Index

# (Index continued)

# (Index continued)

www.houstonwilderness.org